ALYS  A

Mending Tomorrow

CHOOSING HOPE, FINDING WHOLENESS

FIRST EDITION

Unless otherwise identified, Scripture quotations are taken from the Holy Bible, New Living Translation, copyright 1996, 2004. Used by permission of Tyndale House Publishers, Wheaton, Illinois 60189. All rights reserved.

Scripture quotations marked ESV are taken from The Holy Bible, English Standard Version® (ESV®), copyright © 2001 by Crossway, a publishing ministry of Good News Publishers. Used by permission. All rights reserved.

Scripture quotations marked KJV are taken from the King James Version. Public domain. NIV (New International Version 2010) Scripture marked NIV are taken from THE HOLY BIBLE, NEW INTERNATIONAL VERSION®, NIV®. Copyright © 1973, 1978, 1984, 2010 by Biblica, Inc.™ www.xulonpress.com.

Editor: Allison Armerding | www.allisonarmerding.com
Cover Design: © Yvonne Parks | www.pearcreative.ca
Interior Design: © Renee Evans | reneeevansdesign.com

ISBN: 978-1-942306-18-4
LCCN: 2015919201

Printed in the United States
www.newtypepublishing.com

N|T NEWTYPE

Endorsements

There's a certain power in being taught by someone who has lived the reality of the theme they seek to teach on. That's exactly why Alyssa Quilala's brave, beautiful book will impact many lives so deeply. In *Mending Tomorrow*, she speaks with an inspiring mix of vulnerability and authority, reminding us how to remind ourselves of the goodness of God, even as we walk through the valley of shadows. Her willingness to let us inside their story, and Chris Quilala's poignant chapter too, are a huge blessing. This book will help so many people who have lost little ones and loved ones—and help make better worshippers of us all.

MATT REDMAN
Singer, Songwriter, UK

I am in awe of Alyssa's courage and determination to pursue the goodness of God throughout her experience of walking through such loss. In *Mending Tomorrow*, Alyssa shares her own stories and core beliefs on what worship looks like, even in the depths of pain. She encourages us to pursue hope and to have faith in God's Word, though we may not yet see the light in the tunnel we are journeying through. This message is a healing read that is full of promise and the love of the Father.

KARI JOBE
Singer, Songwriter

I am so grateful that Alyssa has written a book about her experience of learning to walk with God in the midst of loss and unanswered questions. She has opened up her life and allowed us to walk the journey with her in a real and honest way so that others facing hard situations may experience the same strength, hope, and love she experienced found only in God. The truths in *Mending Tomorrow* will reveal the heart of a good Father who draws close to us in our loss and pain.

BANNING LIEBSCHER
Jesus Culture Director

Dedication

Chris—"Mon choix, mon amour." Every day spent with you has been more beautiful than the last. You are who you say you are.

Ella, Aria, and Liv—my girls, my precious angels, my heart. Parenting you all is the most invigorating life experience, and my days are full of joy just looking into your bright eyes!

Jet—Carrying you for almost 9 months was one of the greatest privileges of my life. You opened my eyes. I can't wait to hold you again, my baby blue.

M. Earl Johnson and James Grubbs—It may seem odd to thank you in this book, as I didn't know either of you. Thank you for the way you invested in your family while you were here. The principles of the goodness of God that you invested in the people around you will never be forgotten. When you left for heaven, Chris and I watched your family members grieve in the most holy and beautiful way. When Jethro left for heaven, your family was the example we needed to help us heal. You've done far more for our lives than I would have ever realized. Thank you for your legacy.

Contents

Foreword

BY BILL JOHNSON

Mending Tomorrow: Choosing Hope, Finding Wholeness is a very powerful book. You won't find a cheap attempt at giving classroom theories on overcoming pain. Neither will you read of the "five keys to your breakthrough" or some other attempt to train us in mental gymnastics and formulas to come into victory. While I believe in the principles that lead us out of tragedy into triumph, I am also convinced that Alyssa Quilala takes us on a journey where we discover the real treasure—the Father. Prepare yourself to embark on the expedition of your life. This story is extremely intimate and truthful, and at times painful, but always redemptive.

Psalm 84:5 has become especially dear to me of late. It reads, *"As they pass through the valley of weeping, they make it a spring; the rain also covers it with pools."* If ever I've seen a book that illustrated this profound truth, it is this one. The Quilalas never denied their pain, nor did they pretend all was well when it wasn't. There were tears...many of them. But because they drew near to God, instead of running from Him with accusation, anger, and resentment, they saw the fulfillment of this prophetic passage—tears became springs.

Tears are places of loss, disappointment, and pain. Springs are places of refreshing. God did what only He can do, when they did what they knew to do. They gave Him honor and thanks in spite of loss. Soon, the barren place upon which they stood became a spring of refreshing.

How can this be? How can our greatest loss become the place of our greatest gain? This mystery is so wonderful and glorious that in it we become enabled to embrace a lifestyle of thanksgiving and praise regardless of circumstances. Because He always remains the same, it is the only logical way for the believer to live.

But their story doesn't end with springs of refreshing. The conclusion is that the "rain also covers it with pools." Not only has this family turned their tears into springs—God has added His portion called *the rains of blessing, favor, and increase to their lives.* Their place of greatest inadequacy has become their place of greatest authority.

We all want the blessing of the Lord. But few draw near to the Father after there has been great loss. If I can't be faithful in disappointment, I can't be trusted with the blessings for which I have prayed. This is the reality of those who pursue all that God has for us in this lifetime.

I was in the hospital room with the Quilalas and many mutual friends, praying for the God of mercy to bring about a miracle of resurrection for their baby son, Jethro. At one point, Chris brought Jet to me. As he placed him into my arms, I looked into Chris's eyes. They were not filled with panic or fear. They were filled with hope, and I knew this was to be one of the most significant moments of my life. It was. I held the body of this beautiful boy, speaking life, calling on the One who is perfectly faithful in all He does to come and restore.

As you know by now, Jet did not come back from the dead. But something happened to many of us in that room. We caught a glimpse of eternity, as well as the very present resurrection power of Jesus. We now live aware that we were born for much more than we've seen. The power of His resurrection has touched our souls, and we will never be the same.

Join us in this wonderful journey and see what God might give you to shape the world around you for His name's sake.

BILL JOHNSON

Senior Pastor of Bethel Church, Redding, CA
Author of *When Heaven Invades Earth* and *Hosting the Presence*

Chapter 1

TRAUMA AND TRUST

"O God my rock," I cry, "Why have you forgotten me? Why must I wander around in grief, oppressed by my enemies?"

PSALM 42:9

This is a book about responses, and that means it's also a book about questions. It's not so much about the questions we ask of our lives: "Why did that happen? What do I want? Will I get it?" It's about the questions our lives, and the Author of our lives, ask of us. These questions, embedded in our experiences, ask, "How did that affect you? What are you going to do about it? What *should* you do about it?"

Life's questions become particularly poignant and powerful when we experience pain and loss. When things are taken from us or done to us without our permission or control, it's tempting to get stuck in *our* questions. We can obsess over the whys and the would-haves for a long time and avoid coming to terms with the questions that actually matter: "What am I going to do? How am I going to respond to this?"

We always get to choose how we're going to respond to life's questions. In many ways, that's the only choice we really have. Embracing that truth is the first step toward health, wholeness, and everything good in life. Ultimately, it is the key to resilience, to enduring and growing through difficulties rather than being destroyed by them. Austrian psychiatrist Viktor Frankl, who lost his entire family during the Holocaust and survived six months in a concentration camp, described the power of embracing this truth in his book, *Man's Search for Meaning*:

> We had to learn...that it did not really matter what we expected from life, but rather, what life expected from us. We needed to stop asking about the meaning of life, and instead to think of ourselves as those who were being questioned by life—daily and hourly. Our answer must consist, not in talk and meditation, but in right action and in right conduct. Life ultimately means taking the responsibility to find the right answer to its problems and to fulfill the tasks which it constantly sets for each individual.[1]

---

[1] Viktor Frankl, *Man's Search for Meaning* (Boston: Beacon Press, 1992), 85.

We'll never find the right answers in life until we find and understand the right questions. But we won't even start looking for the right questions if we don't know that responding well to them is what "life ultimately means." We either choose to become, or resist becoming, the people God created us to be as we respond to life's questions.

Each human story is unique, and life will ask its questions of us at different times and in different ways. However, we can be sure we will all be asked about the same important things, for the same Author is behind our stories. In the pages ahead, I offer you the lessons I have been learning as I respond to some of the questions life has asked of me—all in the hope of encouraging you as you respond to the questions life is asking of you.

THE HARDEST QUESTION

On December 1, 2014, life asked me the hardest question I've ever been asked.

It began that afternoon, when a fleeting thought crossed my mind.

Something's different.

I looked down at my pregnant belly strapped beneath my seatbelt. My husband, Chris, sat beside me in the driver's seat, while our daughters, almost-five-year-old Ella and twenty-one-month-old Aria, giggled and munched on snacks in their car seats behind us. Though we had just celebrated several days of Thanksgiving festivities with family and friends, we were excited to be on our way to Redding, California for our annual "Friendsgiving" dinner.

Suddenly, I realized what was bothering me.

Jet hasn't kicked me yet.

The much-anticipated due date of our son, Jethro Dylan Quilala—Jet—was only four weeks away. The pregnancy had been completely normal. Just days ago at a checkup, my doctor had announced that Jet's heart was perfectly strong, his growth progress was excellent, and there was nothing to be concerned about. Yet today, it was already two in the afternoon, and I hadn't felt him move.

I usually feel him by now.

Cries from the back seat interrupted my thoughts. Aria wanted more snacks, and Ella, for the umpteenth time, was calling, "Are we there, yet?" Distracted, I pushed Jet's unusual stillness aside.

By late evening, however, I couldn't ignore the fact that I hadn't felt Jet move all day. I finally mentioned it to Chris. For the next half hour, we tried everything that usually roused Jet into action—drinking cold water, massaging my belly, and having Chris sing songs close to my belly. Still nothing.

Finally, Chris looked at me and asked, "Should we go check it out?"

I hesitated, then nodded. "I'm sure he's fine...but just to be safe."

It was long after midnight when we arrived the ER. They immediately sent us straight to Labor and Delivery. I positioned myself on the exam room bed and watched as a nurse squeezed gel onto my stomach and pressed it with the Doppler probe. I couldn't help holding my breath as I waited to hear Jet's heartbeat—the heartbeat I had heard only days ago, beating hard and fast.

Tonight, I waited...and waited. As the seconds ticked by, we heard only silence.

The nurse shook her head and looked up at me, her eyes full of pity. "I can't find a heartbeat, but there can be other reasons for that. I'll page the doctor on call to perform an ultrasound."

I lay on the table, still hardly daring to breathe, trying to suppress the wave of panic that was rising inside me. *She can't find a heartbeat.*

Moments later, the doctor came in and quietly began the ultrasound process I had experienced so many times. Images of Jet began to appear on the monitor screen. However, this time the images were different. I saw an utterly still baby on the monitor—no heartbeat, no squirming.

The doctor said, "I'm so sorry. This confirms our fears. Your son has no heartbeat and no movement."

"No, no, no, no!" The sobs burst from me as Chris

squeezed my hand. "We just had him checked the other day! Everything was perfect."

"This just happens sometimes," the doctor said softly, laying the probe down and wiping the gel off my belly with a paper towel. "You'll need to be induced. You can start immediately, or go home and come back in the morning. I'll give you some time to talk it over." With a sigh, he stood and left the room.

I sat up, cradling my bulging belly, and cried as I had never cried before. Loud, groaning sobs full of anguish wracked my body. Chris held me as his tears mingled with mine.

It was simply too much to take in. Impossible. How could the fully formed, healthy, very-much-alive boy who had been kicking me only yesterday have no heartbeat? How could I have carried life inside me for eight months and suddenly be carrying...death?

Numb and speechless, Chris and I held on to each other in that room for forty-five minutes, unable to make any decisions. Finally, we agreed to go home, inform our friends and family, and try to rest.

Members of our family met us at our house and stayed awake with us through the night. We just held each other and cried endlessly. Finally, morning arrived, as did more family members and some of our closest friends, including Bill and Beni Johnson, and Brian and Jenn Johnson. Bill Johnson is a spiritual father in our lives, and a father of faith who has seen God do many amazing miracles—including seeing babies who were born alive after having been declared dead in the womb. With sober confidence, Bill looked at Chris and me and said, "It's not over." He then began leading everyone in prayer for Jet's life.

Songs of praise, led by Brian and Jenn, soon mingled with the prayers. Chris and I couldn't help but continue to weep, but with all the strength we had, we lifted our broken voices in praise to God and agreed with the declarations of life over our son.

After a time, Bill saw how overwhelmed and exhausted I was, and put a hand on my shoulder. "You don't need to carry this, Alyssa," he said quietly. "Carry hope. Holding on to hope in the middle of despair is what gives God the room to move. But you don't have to press in for the miracle; you only need to be the mother of the miracle."

Finally, around 10 a.m., we decided to go to the hospital. Everyone in the room offered to accompany us and continue with worship there. Half an hour later, I was lying in a hospital bed, waiting for the induction drugs to kick in and wondering vaguely how long it would take to deliver my son's body.

The answer turned out to be *forty hours*. A forty-hour nightmare. A forty-hour vigil.

In those forty hours, I experienced the worst physical, mental, and emotional pain of my life. Along with labor contractions, powerful emotions continuously built and crested over me as I struggled to take in the excruciating reality of what was happening. Shock and disbelief. Anger. The sickening heaviness of death.

Yet in those hours of anguish, our community continued to surround me and raise their hands and voices to God in prayer, praise, and worship. With words of hope, comfort, and faith, they changed the atmosphere in the room. Like the friends of the paralytic who lowered him through the roof to Jesus, our community gave us their strength and led us into the presence of God, praying the prayers I couldn't pray and singing the songs I couldn't sing.

Finally, I pushed for the last time. Moments later, the doctor handed me the tiny, limp body of my son, swaddled in a blanket. Chris put his head to mine as we gazed down into the face of Jethro Dylan Quilala.

He was perfect. Breathtaking. He had his father's curly dark hair, and his sweet red mouth, shaped just like mine, was open, as though he was breathing. It felt just like the two times before, when I had taken each of our baby girls in my arms for the first time and beheld their beautiful faces.

But our love and wonder for Jet was soon mingled with the unbearable weight of the truth. He was gone. We had met him at last, only to say goodbye.

MY TURN

The continued waves of support, love, prayer, and help from our family and church community carried Chris and me as we made funeral arrangements for Jet and planned his memorial service. At the service, we worshiped together again, declaring God's goodness and faithfulness over us. And then, we went home, and I had to start facing the hardest question.

The question was, "Will you trust God in the midst of trauma and loss?"

My loved ones had helped answer that question for me in my living room, at the hospital, and at my son's memorial. Now I had to respond to it on my own, without being able to simply follow in their wake. And while I had every intention of responding with a strong "Yes," I found myself confronting a new challenge.

The difficulty for me did not lie in accepting Jet's death. I mourned it deeply, but I can honestly say I never felt anger or blame toward God. On several occasions following the memorial, someone made a comment to me about God "taking" my son, and I instantly responded, "God isn't a baby killer. He didn't 'take' my son. My boy was stolen, but God provided an everlasting eternity to bring restoration to a terrible situation!"

The challenge was simply that my mind and body were experiencing all the effects of trauma.

Thus, whenever I began to think about the future, I became paralyzed with panic. It was like a door slammed in my head—I just couldn't go there. Instead, my mind began to race with crazy, anxious thoughts. Would God allow me to experience trauma like this in the future? Did He really know what I was capable of surviving? Did He really want to fill my life with favor? What if I didn't want the favor of God, if it required me to go through loss like this? Had I done something wrong? Was He angry with me?

For the most part, I knew these questions were on the irrational side, so I kept trying to push them aside and ignore them. I busied myself with mom duties and went through the motions of reading my Bible, worshipping, going to church, and doing other activities I hoped would help me feel like me again. Yet whenever anyone mentioned words like "hope" or "everything working out for good" to me, I found myself cringing as though they were swear words. How could I possibly have any new hope when the one thing I hoped most for didn't happen? How could anything be "good" except having my son back, which was never to be? A few times, I got so irritated by people's well-meaning Bible verses and encouragements that I considered punching them in the face. Truths I had always quoted and believed were turning into triggers for my pain.

Pushing my anxiety away did nothing to ease it. Instead of gradually dissipating as I had expected, the insomnia I had experienced every night since I left the hospital got worse. When I could sleep, I woke up with TMJ from all the tension in my jaw. Then one day, I came down with what I thought was a gastrointestinal infection. I was feverish, my heart was racing, and I was feeling a lot of pain and pressure in my abdomen. I went to the ER, had multiple tests to find the problem, and was told, "Your body has the symptoms of an infection, but you don't have one. Nothing is wrong with you. You're perfectly healthy. Given what you've just gone through, however, we think you're probably dealing with symptoms of chronic fatigue syndrome and PTSD. The stress you're carrying is causing your body to attack itself."

Those words finally flipped the switch for me to see how "not okay" I really was. I had been telling myself I was answering the hard question, but the fact that my body was telling me I was sick when I wasn't told me that fear was currently winning over trust.

I needed to encounter God. I needed to be delivered of my fears so my ravaged mind and heart could heal and trust Him again.

The first way to restore trust, I decided, was to start looking at the evidence of His trustworthiness. I made a commitment to read the Word and remind myself of the goodness of God until my thoughts and emotions began to align with and experience the truth. Day after day, I searched the

Bible for answers, for the verses I needed to hear. And slowly and quietly, God met me there. Verse after verse and story after story seemed to wind soothing bandages around the gaping wounds in my soul. Gradually, I noticed that the pain lessened and my mind became more aware of His heart of love towards me. My sense of abandonment gave way to the consciousness that God hadn't missed a thing. He not only saw my pain; He felt it. In my suffering, He was closer to me than ever before. I experienced the truth of Psalm 34:18: "The LORD is near to the brokenhearted and saves the crushed in spirit" (ESV).

In this process, I discovered a profound truth. Coming to know how God feels about our pain is the biggest reason we'll ever find to trust Him. So many of us live with a sense that God is distant in our pain, which is the exact opposite of the truth. We cannot begin to fathom how much He cares and how fully He is *with us* as we suffer. He is the God of *compassion*—the very word means "to suffer with." And He is Immanuel, "God with us." Experiencing His "withness" silences the torment of the "whys." The mystery of what we can't know or understand fades in the light of what we can know with utmost certainty—that He is here. And because He suffers with us, we can be healed.

So many of us shut down our emotions and prevent our own healing because we don't know that God cares about everything we're feeling. Or we try to manufacture emotions of joy and hope because we know that's what we're "supposed to do." But in this season of rebuilding trust, I came to see that my job in healing was simply to go to Him as I was. He cared about every nuance of my emotions and knew exactly how to restore my soul.

LET GO, MY SOUL

Author Ally Condie wrote, "In the end you can't always choose what you keep. You can only choose how you let it go."[2] Letting go is, in many ways, the essence of trust. In Psalm 46:10, the Lord says, "Be still and know that I am God." The Hebrew word translated "be still" can also be translated "let go." If we want to know that He is God in our lives, we must let go of everything else we're holding on to. That said, letting go is truly an act of grace. We need God's help to release the things we grip so hard in our need to understand and control our circumstances.

As God, day by day, strengthened my trust in Him, He gave me the grace to let go—of the questions, of hurt, bitterness, and offense, of false expectations for my healing process. And with each letting go, I felt His love and compassion saturate my heart more and more.

Then one day, several weeks into this "letting go" process, I heard the Lord's still, small voice ask me, "Is it well with your soul now?"

One of the songs suggested by our friends and family to be sung at Jet's memorial service was Kristene DiMarco's version of "It Is Well." When I saw it on the list, I froze. Could I really sing the refrain "It is well with my soul" over and over? And then there was the bridge:

Let go, my soul, and trust in Him—

The waves and wind still know His name.

I knew I couldn't sing those words. It was definitely *not* well with my soul, and I had no idea how to let go and trust God. I told them, somewhat harshly, to take the song off the list.

But the day God reminded me of that song, I knew I was in a different place. I was coming to know God in a way I'd never known Him before (one of the gifts for which I can thank my beautiful son) and I could sincerely say, "Let go, my soul, and trust in Him." I was finally answering the hard question with a "Yes" that came from my whole being.

I had also, incidentally, discovered the story of the original hymn "It Is Well," written in 1873 by Horatio Spafford. If you're not familiar with the story, you should know that this beloved hymn was penned after the tragic loss of Spafford's children. Spafford sent his wife and four daughters to England on a boat, which collided with another ship midway across the Atlantic and sank. He received

---

[2] Ally Condie, *Crossed*, (New York: Penguin Young Readers Group, 2013), 21.

a telegram from his wife that read, "Saved alone." Some time later, Spafford made the same voyage, and as he reached the place where his daughters had drowned, he looked across the crashing washes and wrote the powerful words of hope that have been sung for generations: "Whatever my lot, Thou has taught me to say, 'It is well, it is well with my 'soul.'"

When I heard this story, I thought, *If this man could lose his precious children and still trust God, then I will too.* And on that day, when He asked me, it only took me a moment to know the answer.

"Yes, Lord," I whispered. "It is well with my soul."

Chapter 2

THE STING AND THE HONEY

---

*The Lord God is my Strength, my personal bravery,
and my invincible army; He makes my feet like
hind's feet and will make me to walk [not to stand
still in terror, but to walk] and make [spiritual]
progress upon my high places [of trouble, suffering, or responsibility]!*

HABAKKUK 3:19 AMP

The Bible is clear about the attitude we're supposed to take toward tragedy, trials, and pain. "Here on earth you will have many trials and sorrows," Jesus promises, "But take heart, because I have overcome the world" (John 16:33). Similarly, James says, "When troubles come your way, consider it an opportunity for great joy. For you know that when your faith is tested, your endurance has a chance to grow" (James 1:2-3). In short, we shouldn't be surprised by tragedy, but should see it as a way for more positive things to come into our lives.

That sounds great on paper, but doing it is utterly daunting. How on earth are we supposed to turn negatives into positives?

Losing Jet opened my eyes to how many people think that "counting it all joy" means doing whatever you can to put a positive spin on something negative—to the point of creating "positives" that aren't really positive at all.

"At least it wasn't one of your daughters," one well-meaning person told me. "It would be much harder if one of them had died."

All I can say is that I'm glad I held my tongue in that moment, because if I hadn't, it wouldn't have been pretty.

Turning negatives into positives doesn't mean trying to twist our brains so we can somehow see that a negative isn't a negative. It has to do with responding to the negative in a way that creates a positive result.

As you might imagine, this negative-positive dilemma was at the heart of my journey to restore trust in God after losing Jet. So let me go back and share a few more details of my emotional process and how I learned what it meant to count loss as an opportunity for joy.

VALIDATING THE NEGATIVE

In the weeks following Jet's memorial, I experienced what so many experience after a loss. The time of public grieving ended. The donated meals, condolences, and sympathy cards stopped arriving. Everyone outside our closest circle of relationships returned to business as usual...just as I was entering the actual process of grieving myself. It seemed that most of the world around me stopped feeling my pain right when I was starting to *really* feel it.

None of us likes to feel alone in our pain, or be treated as though our pain doesn't matter. We crave validation, empathy, and connection. We feel inadequate to deal with the powerful emotions of anger, sadness, and fear, terrified that they will crush us, or that the world around us will expect us to move on and be okay when we're not. Being honest with ourselves about those needs, however, is difficult. Consciously or unconsciously, we often end up trying to meet them in ways that are counterproductive.

I know some people try to manage pain by hiding it, bottling it up, and trying to put a brave, happy face on things. If you're a Christian leader, you often feel pressure to show everyone that you're "counting it all joy" by never revealing that you're experiencing painful emotions.

To me, however, hiding my feelings of grief felt like being fake. I couldn't do it. Instead, I started wearing this "wounded" attitude around like a cloak wherever I went. I wanted everyone to know that something terrible had happened to me, and that I was hurting. I couldn't stop to tell my story of woe to everyone, however, so I communicated in other ways. When the Starbucks barista smiled at me, I glared back at her. If someone told me, "Have a great day!" I made a snide remark. I ignored text messages from friends and family members trying to encourage me. Anytime the world around me sent a message that life was good and everything was okay, I had to shoot it down in some way. I wanted to scream, "Things are NOT OKAY!"

The more I reacted in these ways, the more I felt justified in doing so. My pain, I felt, gave me permission to act however I needed in order to make the world around me share my pain. I wanted everyone to walk on eggshells around me, to respect the "bubble" I was creating around my hurt in order to keep it from being dismissed, or even helped. I refused to act like my negative experience was not negative, and I wanted the world to agree with me about how negative it was.

The more I worked to get my world to protect and validate my pain, however, the more my pain became all I could think about. Slowly, before I could realize what was happening, I had become the center of my own attention. Though I continued to go through the motions of my responsibilities as a wife and mother, I became almost totally disconnected from everyone around me, passing through my days in a stupefied, "zombied" state.

I was walking through the house in this "zombie" demeanor one morning when my daughter, Ella, who is as sassy as can be and likes to call things exactly as they are, stopped me in my tracks. She looked straight up at me and asked, "If you're having a bad day, why do I have to have a bad day too?"

I was stunned, then offended. "You can have a good day even if I'm sad," I retorted. "My feelings don't change your feelings."

Ella's pointed glare didn't budge. "Well, I'm over here trying to laugh and smile," she said, " but every time I see your grumpy face it makes me feel grumpy too."

I was speechless. I had just been "told" by a five-year-old!

Ella's confrontation snapped me out of my pity party. I saw that the way I was dealing with my pain was hurting the people I loved most. I was reacting to the loss of my son in a way that deprived my beautiful daughters of the mother they needed. My feelings *did* affect their feelings. I was releasing a toxic poison into my environment, which my daughter automatically recognized and felt.

My negative experience, I realized, didn't give me permission to act however I wanted. I had to take responsibility for the way I was dealing with my pain and change my approach. I wasn't, as I had told myself, being "real" about my pain by walking around like a zombie. I was actually trying to force everyone in my world to deal with my feelings instead of dealing with them myself.

So how was I supposed to respond to my negative feelings authentically and responsibly? How could I begin to create a healthy emotional environment and set a positive example of emotional responsibility for my daughters?

THE ONE WHO CAN HANDLE IT

I knew the only answer was to begin processing this dilemma with God. Doing so meant being vulnerable and trusting Him, which, again, I had not been finding terribly easy. But between Ella's confrontation and the stress-related health issues I was dealing with, I was desperate to get in a better place. So I gathered my courage and made that commitment to seek the Lord in the Word and prayer.

One of the Scriptures that ministered deeply to me in this season was Psalm 56:8:

You keep track of all my sorrows.

You have collected all my tears in your bottle.

You have recorded each one in your book.

When I first understood what this verse was saying, it hit me that I had been trying to get everyone around me to validate how "not okay" my negative situation was, while holding myself back from the one Person who was validating that experience so thoroughly that He was collecting every one of my tears and journaling about it! The revelation that He knew absolutely everything I was going through and cared about it suddenly lifted me out of this exhausting double duty of trying to validate my own pain while being in it. It was as though He was saying, "I know how bad it is. It's so bad, in fact, that only I can fix it. Only I can bear the full weight of this grief for you. So let me have it."

I ended up spending a lot of time in the Psalms as I began to learn to let God carry my pain. If you read the Psalms, you can't help but notice all the emotional honesty of the Psalmist. Again and again, he bares his soul, expressing the full range of human emotion around pain—blazing anger, paralyzing terror, crippling sorrow. Many of us don't like to camp out in these verses. We like to breeze through them and get to the triumphant declarations of praise and hope. But walking through my own journey of pain helped me appreciate just how powerful it is that the Psalmist could be so raw and real with God. It's hard to be real with someone when we're not sure they can handle it. The Psalmist's ability to tell God, "This really sucks, and here's why," is actually an expression of faith that God fully understands, deeply cares, and will never judge or punish us in our pain. He not only can handle it—He's the only One who can handle it.

JOY AND GRATITUDE

Until we see the One who can handle our pain, I'm not sure any of us can really be free from fixating on it and letting it consume our world. The intensity of pain naturally commands our attention. Pain can turn us into the worst version of ourselves by diverting our gaze from everything good to everything that hurts, contracting our focus inward on ourselves. Thankfully, as I began to pour out my questions, emotions, and tears to Him, the selfish focus I had become trapped in was broken. Now I was able to look at Him instead of myself. This posture began to stretch open my field of vision, not only to see God and His goodness more clearly, but also to see all the good things in my life that I had been ignoring or unable to appreciate while focusing on my pain.

While it's true that we can't pretend that a negative is actually a positive, it's also true that a negative doesn't cancel out the other positive things in our lives. Losing Jet didn't take away the fact that I still had an amazing husband, two darling, vivacious daughters, dear friends and family, and a wonderful community. The good things that had filled our lives before our loss remained in our lives.

One of the reasons emotional bitterness is actually a sin is that it leads us to neglect and even scorn God's blessings. It turns our pain into an idol. I didn't just need to apologize to my daughter when she called me on my attitude—I needed to repent for stubbornly insisting that my loss was now the most important thing in my life. In my search for validation, I had started down the dangerous road of elevating my negative experience above everything else, even God. Thankfully, my no-nonsense daughter and the truth of the Scriptures help me put my negative experience back in a proper context.

With the positive things in my life back in view, I was able to begin doing "God's will" described in

1 Thessalonians 5:16-18: "Always be joyful. Never stop praying. Be thankful in all circumstances, for this is God's will for you who belong to Christ Jesus." A lot of people trip over these commands, wondering how it's possible to rejoice and be thankful even when they feel awful. But rejoicing and thankfulness are not emotional responses; they are acts of the will that turn your focus toward God and His goodness in your life. You can declare God's goodness, count your blessings, sing praises, and even jump and dance in response to God's goodness without "feeling" it. If you do these things long enough, however, the reality of His goodness will spill over into your emotions and bring feelings of joy and gratitude. We cultivate healthy emotions by choosing where to put our focus.

REACHING OUT

It was truly remarkable for me to watch how my world responded to an Alyssa who started showing up and declaring the goodness of God with a genuine smile on her face, even through tears. I wasn't too surprised by how happy Chris, Ella, and Aria were to have the grumpy zombie out of the house. But as person after person reached out to tell me how I was giving them hope and courage and causing them to praise God in their own painful situations, I grew increasingly amazed.

Seeing the "ripple effect" I was creating around me helped me understand just how powerful it was to make that simple shift in focus from my pain to God. I felt powerful in a new way. When I was wearing my "wounded" cloak everywhere, I was trying to feel powerful by coercing sympathetic responses from people. But when I began looking to God and His Word, it was as though He gave me a new cloak of strength to wear. I didn't need to try to feel powerful; I was powerful through Him. I began to get excited about using this new strength to bless others, to give away the "positive" that was coming into my life through this healthy response to my negative. As if in response to my changed attitude, opportunities to minister to people began to increase, and one by one I stepped into them.

Then, four months after losing Jet, I received a phone call from the husband of a friend from our church. He told me they had just gone in for their 34-week neonatal checkup and learned that that their baby, a boy, had no heartbeat. Was I willing, he wanted to know, to come to the hospital and be with them during the induced delivery?

There was not a doubt in my mind that being in that hospital room with my friend would be *excruciating*. But I knew if I couldn't be there for her in this situation, it would mean that I was rejecting the next step in my healing journey, that I was putting a cap on this new strength flowing through my life. The woman I was before losing Jet would have gone to the hospital and supported her friend. I wanted the woman I was becoming after losing

Jet not only to go, but to be even more effective in offering comfort because of what I had suffered. I wanted to be able to give more after losing Jet, not less. I stayed with my friend through the entire ordeal. I saw her take a baby boy with no breath into her arms, just as I had done. I gave everything I had in prayers of faith and words of comfort. And miraculously, I did it without shedding single tear.

When I got back home, of course, I knew I had to face the reality of having essentially just relived the worst experience of my life. I stayed in the house for two days, weeping and pouring out my heart to the Lord. But this grieving was far different than the grief of four months before. I knew where to go with the pain. And after my tears were shed, I gave thanks to God for His faithfulness, and for my beautiful son, who had given me the chance to become a stronger, more compassionate woman than before.

THE POWER TO CHOOSE

There's a Swedish proverb that goes, "The bee has a sting, but honey too." It's a metaphor for how life comes to us. We don't get to separate the negatives from the positives. If we want to live life to the full, then we have to develop the capacity to embrace it fully—pain and pleasure, bitter and sweet. Both the sting and the honey can make us stronger if we learn to respond well to them.

I used to fantasize about a futuristic world in which a screen would pop up every morning the moment I opened my eyes, and I would be able to preset the mode of my day. Depending on the day, I could choose, "calm, contemplative, easy laughter," "adventurous, inspiring," or "romantic, restful." Then, no matter what happened, whether my kids were grouchy or I got stuck in traffic, I could relax, knowing that my day would still turn out perfectly because I had already "hacked" it to do so.

Though manipulating our circumstances to perfection is an unrealistic fantasy, my journey of emotional healing has convinced me that none of us needs to be ruled by our circumstances. We all have the power to choose our responses and cultivate healthy emotions by taking every negative to God and focusing on His overwhelmingly positive goodness. We can take every sting to the Holy Spirit and let Him make life sweet, even in its pain.

Chapter 3

THROUGH THE PAIN

---

*"They do not fear bad news; they confidently
trust the Lord to care for them."*

PSALM 112:7

Before we lost Jet, I never really knew what it
was like to experience high levels of anxiety. As
a mother, I was naturally watchful over things
like my daughters' health, nutrition, safety, and
supervision. However, I rarely troubled myself by
imagining possible dangers or worst-case scenarios.

In those weeks when I was post-traumatic,
however, it was a different story. My once safe
and secure life suddenly seemed full of terrifying
dangers, and thinking about any one of them for
very long was enough to trigger a panic attack.
One of the thoughts that fueled my continued
insomnia was this: "If my son can die for absolutely
no medically known reason, then any one of my
children could easily die without explanation too."
Night after night, an unshakable premonition kept

me on edge, waiting to hear one of my girls start screaming. I put a baby monitor beside my bed because their room isn't close to the master bedroom. If I heard so much as a cough, I immediately began imagining that whoever had coughed had lung cancer. I'd spin out this wild idea in my mind until it had become a horrific saga of us living for months in the hospital, watching as our daughter wasted away and finally died with one last painful gasp.

It sounds crazy, I know. But this is fear. Fear will take one bad experience and hijack your brain into making that experience the new rule for what you should expect in life. As irrational as fear is, it can be hard to resist. The thing you never dreamed would happen happened, and it hurt—a lot. As a result, all your senses, discernment, and coping mechanisms are scrambled. Everything in you is on high alert, geared up to sound the alarm if anything threatens to bring that kind of pain into your world again.

THE LESSON OF THE GARDEN

It's tempting to wish that the fear and anxiety spiked by a painful experience will naturally calm down, and our thoughts and emotions will return to a healthy baseline on their own. But every healing process, whether physical, mental, emotional, or spiritual, requires us to make choices that enable that process to be successful. If you get a cut, cleaning and bandaging it will protect the cut while it heals. If you leave the cut exposed, you could get an infection that might actually threaten your life.

In the same way, if you don't address fear and anxiety after a bad experience, they will end up causing just as many problems, if not more, than the thing that triggered them. If you've gone through counseling or any form of inner healing, then you probably know this well. Every major issue people struggle with in life—addictions, fear of intimacy, crippling insecurity, shame and guilt— all stem from painful experiences that never healed properly. And the reason they didn't heal properly is that the person listened to fear and arranged their whole reality around trying to avoid or protect themselves from pain, using anything but God.

I'm convinced that God is the only source of healing in the universe. He's the only One who offers us another response to pain and fear that not only restores us fully, but makes us more resilient on the other side of them. The problem is that most of us have a really hard time going to God in our pain—a problem we can trace all the way back to the garden.

As far as we can tell, Adam and Eve never knew pain and fear until they sinned. Sin opened the door to everything painful in the world—disease, sickness, pain in childbirth, relational strife, cruelty, natural disasters, and more. But these effects came after Adam and Eve experienced what is arguably the most intolerable pain humans can experience: the pain of shame and guilt. The pain of shame drove Adam and Eve to hide from God. The pain of guilt drove them to try and shift the blame on to someone else. These two fear-based responses to pain—hiding and blame-shifting—have been the classic human responses to pain ever since.

Above all, humanity has learned to hide from and blame God. Whether our pain is the consequence of our own sin or the consequence of living in a fallen, broken world, the lesson it teaches us is that we do not live in a safe place, and a lot of people think this means the Person running the show is either out to lunch, or not good. "How could a good God allow us to make such a mess of things?" they ask. "Why doesn't He stop all these bad things from happening?" While it's natural to ask these questions, the problem is that a lot of people don't believe God has a satisfactory answer to them. So they reject God, seek alternative sources of protection and comfort, and attempt to stay in the driver's seat of their lives. Despite centuries of proof that this approach only leads to bondage and more pain, they keep falling for it.

But God does have an answer to why He's allowed His children to fall and create a world of pain for themselves. Put simply, God intends to reveal Himself as a good Father in the midst of this broken world and draw us into a relationship in which He teaches us how to overcome pain and fear rather than being overcome by them. The only way His answer will make sense, however, is by experiencing it for ourselves. In order to do that, we must invite Him to come into our messy, hurting lives and help us face our pain and fear *with Him.*

A GOOD FATHER

Appropriately, God used an incident with one of my children to help me invite Him into my battle against anxiety.

I was in the living room folding laundry one day when I heard a loud yell.

"Mama, I stuck! Can you help you! I need help you!"

In case you don't speak two-year-old, this is my daughter Aria's way of saying, "I need your help!" I ran to the kitchen and found her standing on the kitchen island, her hands and mouth covered in chocolate. Somehow she had found a way to climb up and get into the forbidden stash of treats, but hadn't realized she wouldn't be able to get down.

Upon seeing the look on my face, Aria's countenance fell. She knew she'd been caught red-handed (or chocolate-handed) doing two things she shouldn't be doing. In a sad, little voice she said, "I sorry, Mama. I need help you."

I helped her down, cleaned her up, had a little talk with her about the dangers of climbing and how she couldn't have chocolate without permission, and put her in a short time-out. Then I returned to the laundry basket and began spiraling through one paranoid "what if" after another in my mind.

What if Aria hadn't called for help? What if she had fallen or hurt herself? I began to wrestle an urge to buy one of those protective bubbles to put Aria in when I couldn't have my eye on her. *Or maybe I could cover every surface of the house in bubble wrap?*

Then the words of a Bible verse surfaced in my mind, interrupting my escalating worry: "So if you sinful people know how to give good gifts to your children, how much more will your heavenly Father give good gifts to those who ask him" (Matthew 7:11).

I began to chew on these words. A new "what if" occurred to me. *What if Aria had come to me first and asked for chocolate?* Immediately, I knew what I would have done. I would have gone in the kitchen and given her some chocolate. There would have been no mess and no danger.

It's true, I thought. *I do know how to give good gifts to my children—and I want them to know that. I never want my children to be afraid of what will happen if they ask me for something. I want them always to know that I have their best interests in mind, and I want to see them get the best!*

Almost as soon as I finished this thought, however, another question popped into my mind. *So, if God knows how to give you good gifts far more than you know how to give them to your girls, why don't you go to Him as much as you want them to come to you? How many times have you gotten stuck because you kept trying to figure it out on your own instead of asking for His help?*

Convicted, I began to pour out my heart to the Lord. I told Him that even though I knew He was a good Father, losing my son kept making me so scared. I didn't know how to deal with my fear and anxiety. I didn't feel safe or protected. I didn't know how to stop bracing myself for another loss. I didn't know how to capture all the paranoid thoughts that were randomly tormenting me day and night.

In response to these confessions, God reminded me of another verse: "For God gave us a spirit not of fear but of power and love and self-control" (2 Timothy 1:7 ESV). In an instant, these words brought my internal world into focus. It was as though God had swung a sword and separated two things that had become confused—my painful experience, and my fear of future pain—and was telling me, "Fear is not the lesson I want you to learn from this bad experience. You have another option, because you have My Spirit inside you—the Spirit of power, love, and self-control. My Spirit gives you the ability to overcome pain and face your future with confidence, knowing that no matter what happens, I'm right here. Never once have you walked alone, and you never will. You can always come to Me."

Seeing that my fear was not God's heart for me caused me to turn a corner in my journey of healing from trauma-related anxiety. Though I continued to experience moments of stress and panic in the following weeks and months, they were shorter and less intense because I knew what to do. Before my mind could get locked in the hamster wheel of scared "what ifs," I stopped and reminded myself not to listen to the spirit of fear. And then I cried out to my Father, as Aria had cried out to me: "I need help You!" Without fail, He spoke truth to my heart and brought peace to my anxious thoughts. My sleep and mood improved, and I stopped feeling like I was going crazy!

GOING THROUGH IT WITH HIM

There is simply *no way* God is not going to come when we cry out for His help. Our Father wants the same thing that I want for my daughters. He wants us to learn to come to Him in everything, for everything, so we can learn to walk in partnership with Him. This is the invitation He makes to us every time He shows up in the midst of our pain and powerlessness.

You can't find a person in the Bible who ended up partnering with God and doing amazing things who didn't have seasons—sometimes, really long seasons—where everything was messy, confusing, painful, stressful, disappointing, devastating, and even downright terrifying. Joseph endured thirteen years in which he was sold into slavery by his brothers, falsely accused, put in prison, and forgotten by those he helped, before the dream God gave him as a young teenager came to pass. Moses was an outcast for forty years before God brought him into his destiny to deliver Israel. David was running for his life from Saul for years before he became king. Yet in every single story, it's clear that these long seasons did something crucial to prepare these people for their destiny. Somewhere in those years of struggle, they all began to invite God into their pain and fear. They found intimacy with God in their pain, and this enabled them to stop running from it, and instead to pass through it with Him. On the other side, each of these people had a testimony about a good God who gave them something through pain that they couldn't have gotten anywhere else. It was more than character. People say "pain builds character," and they are right, *but only if* the pain teaches us to trust and depend on God. Our character is built as we invite God into the pain, allow Him to comfort us, teach us, and empower us to overcome the pain, and move forward from a place of greater intimacy and trust in Him.

Nathan Edwardson, senior pastor of the Stirring Church in Redding, said something in a sermon that captured this point for me so well. "Often times, we do everything in our own power to avoid the pain and suffering in our lives," he said. "Some of us fake it; others medicate it. And yet, there's an encounter with God only found in suffering, a love experienced in the pain, a song written from the depths, an intimacy with God unveiled and known only in the dark night of the soul. There's nothing quite like suffering to bring us face to face with God."

I can say without doubt that the depth of pain I experienced in losing Jet has been met by a depth of intimacy with God that I never imagined before going through that pain. He has encountered me and revealed Himself in the pain in such a way that has silenced all the "why" questions and brought me into a place where I am asking, "What now?"

The answer is that I want this treasure of intimacy with Him to enable me to live without fear of pain and mistakes. I want to be confident that no matter what pain lies ahead, God will meet me there. I want to be brave about exposing my anxious thoughts to Him, assured of His peace and healing, and hopeful that in Him, "that which doesn't kill me only makes me stronger." I want to go to Him in everything, for everything.

FEAR AND FAITH

When it was time for Moses to commission Joshua to lead the people of Israel into the Promised Land, he gave all of them this powerful exhortation: "So be strong and courageous! Do not be afraid and do not panic before them. For the Lord your God will personally go ahead of you. He will neither fail you nor abandon you" (Deuteronomy 31:6).

Forty years before this speech, Israel had sent spies into the Promised Land as they prepared to enter it. Ten out of the twelve spies came back and concluded, "It's too scary. There are giants in the land. We'll never be able to take it." The entire nation listened to their fear, and as a result, God basically said, "You've completely forgotten the One who has gone before you this entire time. Without confidence that I am with you, you have no hope of you winning the battles you need to win to survive in the Promised Land. So here's what's going to happen: I'm going to spend the next forty years raising the next generation to trust Me. You're going to learn to depend on Me for food, water, clothing, health, protection, and everything else." And that's what happened. Only after that generation of fear-infected people had died out and He'd raised a generation that trusted Him did God say, "Let's try this again."

God is passionate and committed to teaching His kids how to overcome fear. Fear is a wet blanket on a blazing fire. It immediately shuts down any potential influence we can have because it seizes the mind into believing things that aren't a reality. It gets us to focus on and trust anything but God. You may have heard the phrase, "Fear is faith in the negative." Fear believes that the promises of God can be stopped, cancelled. We must not give in to fear. We must step into God's promises with strength and courage, confident that He has personally gone before us.

"Gone before us" means that He has already worked out the end of the story, and it's a good ending! It means that even in the lowest and hardest times, He has already fixed things to make it easier for us. He has already protected you from worse things you will never know or see. One of my favorite ways out of an emotional downhill slide is to start thanking God for how He is protecting me in ways that I can't see. It just shuts down all those "why" questions and helps me lean into Him and His promises. The pain will never be the end of the story. There is always triumph on the other side if you go through it with Him.

Chapter 4

THE REASON FOR HOPE

...this hope will not lead to disappointment.
For we know how dearly God loves us,
because he has given us the Holy Spirit
to fill our hearts with his love.

ROMANS 5:5

Growing up as a teenager in Southern California, I often encountered people who assumed I was just another ditzy blonde from the Valley. When I started dating, I was afraid guys would write me off as another flighty California girl, so I felt pressure to impress the guy I was seeing by trying to show him that I was the complete "package" of brains, talent, and looks. Unfortunately, the guys I dated never really seemed impressed by anything but my looks, so after each relationship, I came away feeling even more insecure, more convinced that I wasn't smart or talented enough. Like many of us do, I responded to this insecurity by hiding it and trying even harder to prove myself.

By the time I met my husband, Chris, I was 17 years old and doing my utmost to project a ton of confidence I didn't really feel. He was 25 and ready to find a wife. Somehow, he saw past my immaturity and knew that I was the woman for him. He waited until I was 18 to start pursuing me, and when he did, he took me seriously in a way I had never experienced—a way that felt too good to be true. I didn't believe he could actually value my thoughts and feelings, so whenever he asked for my honest opinion about something, I responded with a sassy or sarcastic joke instead of telling him how I truly felt. To my amazement, he persistently deflected these tactics and insisted that my voice mattered to him. Little by little, I risked telling him tidbits of the depths of my heart. It was scary—I kept bracing myself to be teased by him. But it never happened.

Chris also affirmed my relationship with the Lord in a way no one ever really had. Growing up as the youngest child in a Christian home, my faith was largely part of our family culture, and opportunities for me to stand on my own and speak out of my journey with the Lord weren't especially frequent. Chris expected and challenged me to have a level of maturity in my relationship with the Lord that I could share with him. He wanted to know what I was hearing from God about things in my life or our relationship. This encouraged me to seek the Lord more purposefully, which gradually built my confidence that I could be a spiritual partner and leader alongside Chris.

As Chris continued to invite me to share my heart, validate my words, and pull on my faith, I began to believe, as I had always hoped, that I actually had some brains and something to say. If one person could believe I had something to say, I thought, then maybe others would too. I became curious to discover what else I had inside me. I started to push open the door to my dreams, look at longings I had dismissed, and ask, "Why not?"

Among the dreams I started to take seriously was my dream of being a writer. My confidence in this dream grew until I made a decision: One day, I would write a book. Seven years later, you hold the fruit of that dream in your hands.

YOU MADE ME

In many ways, however, this is not the book I dreamed of writing seven years ago. I never imagined that my first book would be about overcoming loss—a loss that would leave me feeling immensely more insecure than I felt as a teenager.

After losing my son, my confidence was utterly shattered. I couldn't help feeling as though I had let down my husband, my daughters, and my extended family. I was the one who had been carrying Jet's life in my body, and suddenly, his life had ended. Surely that meant I had done something wrong. Despite knowing that this thought was irrational, as every doctor told me there was nothing I could have done differently, I couldn't get over the idea that if I had done more research or been more knowledgeable about pregnancy, I would have been able to save him. I had been very thorough in researching every aspect of my first two pregnancies, and supremely disciplined about doing everything to keep my babies healthy and growing. Throughout my pregnancy with Jet, I felt nothing but confidence that I had all the knowledge, wisdom, and discipline I needed. Yet in the end, they were not enough for my son. Once again, I felt like the silly, young blonde who had probably done something stupid without knowing it.

As he saw me struggling with these feelings of guilt and insecurity, Chris began urging me daily that I hadn't done anything wrong and Jet's death wasn't my fault. I was so buried in pain, however, that his words mostly went in one ear and out the other. Then one day, I was driving down the freeway when one of the songs we chose for Jet's memorial started playing on the car stereo—"My Baby Blue," by Dave Matthews Band:

Confess I'm not quite ready to be left.

Still I know I gave my level best.

You give, you give, to this I can attest

You made me, you made me.

You and me forever, you're my baby blue.[3]

---

[3] Carter Beauford, Stefan Lessard, David J. Matthews, LeRoi Moore, Boyd Tinsley, and Tim Reynolds, "My Baby Blue" (Beam ON Music, 2009)

I had chosen this song because of that one line: "I gave my level best." At the time, I was desperate to say and believe that I had tried my hardest to provide a safe haven for Jet. But as I listened to this song again weeks later, something settled inside me as I heard, "I *know* I gave my level best." The fog of fear cleared in my mind, and I saw the truth: I *had* given my best to my son. I hadn't done anything to harm him.

The line, "You made me," suddenly seemed full of significance as well. I already knew that the experience of losing Jet was shaping me into a different woman, but in that moment, I saw that I could receive it as a gift he had given me, an opportunity to learn and grow and become more of the woman I want to be, the woman I know I am. I understood that allowing grief and insecurity to destroy my confidence and ability to dream were *not* the best way to commemorate his life. Instead, I wanted to keep giving my level best—to God, to my family, and to others—and know that it would be enough. I not only wanted to dream again; I wanted to dream bigger.

KEEPING ON

Proverbs 13:12 says, "Hope deferred makes the heart sick, but a dream fulfilled is a tree of life." We can all relate to that sick feeling in the pit of our stomach when we are let down. It's something we never want to feel again. The temptation in that place is to shut down and stop dreaming about the future. It's just hard to get excited about things to come when all you can think about is how the last time you hoped, you ended up in pain.

As hard as it might be, you *must* choose to hope and dream again on the other side of disappointment. The only other option is to be ruled by the fear of disappointment, which will foster bitterness, unbelief, hopelessness, and resistance to God in your heart. As much as you may want to try to protect yourself from future hurt, the only way you can do that is by pushing away the One who can truly protect you, heal you from disappointment, and lead you to the fulfillment of your dreams and His promises.

Consider Abraham. If there was anyone who could have given into hope deferred and become bitter towards God, it was Abraham. God gave Abraham a promise—a promise that called him to hope—and then waited thirteen years to fulfill that promise. A lot of other people would probably have reached a point where they said, "God, it's been over a decade since You gave me that promise. I officially look like an idiot for believing You would actually give me a son at a hundred years old. All I can see is that You set me up for disappointment. I'm done hoping and believing. Thanks for nothing." But what did Abraham do? "Even when there was no reason for hope, Abraham kept hoping... He was fully convinced that God is able to do whatever he promises" (Romans 4:18, 21). He hoped until his hope was fulfilled.

God is our reason for hope. He wants us to discover that we can hold on to this reason when we can hold on to nothing else—and that when we *do* hold on to Him, wild, unassailable hope will fill our life. God calls us to be people of hope. That's why, when we get around Him, He is always giving us these huge promises, provoking us to dream and hope bigger, and telling us to come to Him with outrageous requests about our dreams. "Keep on asking," He says, "and you will receive what you ask for. Keep on seeking, and you will find. Keep on knocking, and the door will be opened to you" (Matthew 7:7). We must never doubt that God wants to fulfill our dreams, to give us that "tree of life." But we must also recognize that in the waiting, God wants us to become people who can "keep on" no matter what—keep on hoping, keep on believing, and keep on dreaming. He wants us to become resilient to disappointment, able to hope when there is no reason for hope—no reason except Him.

BELIEVE HIM

Refusing to let your experiences of pain and discouragement keep you from dreaming again is the best gift you can give to God. He doesn't care if you mess up, if you're hurt, or if you've been scarred. As I heard Lisa Bevere once say in a message, "Yes, you made a mistake. That does not make you one." He doesn't call you to perfection; He calls you to your potential. And His ability and commitment to fulfill His promises in your life cannot be limited or destroyed by anything you do. He just needs you to trust Him.

The choice to trust God after disappointment, to dream and hope again, not only affects you. It affects everyone around you. Increased faith and hope cannot help but spill over in encouragement. On the other hand, bitterness and hopelessness are just as infectious. If you've ever experienced the toxic environment created by a hopeless, bitter person, you know how discouraging it can be.

As someone who's been on the receiving end of encouragement from one man—my husband—who inspired me to dream, I know how powerful encouragement can be. On the other side of loss, I've decided that I not only want to dream again; I want to be a source of encouragement to others in their dreams.

I once read that Walt Disney was fired by an editor who said he "lacked imagination and had no original ideas." His first animation company went bankrupt, and he was reportedly turned down hundreds of times when he sought financing for Disney World. Today, the average annual revenue of Walt Disney Company is currently US $30 billion.

I don't know about you, but I don't want to be the person who tells the next Walt Disney that they have no imagination! I want to be the person who helps catapult someone into his or her destiny. I want to give them the confidence to dream again.

However, the best encouragement I can give anyone is not to believe me or yourself or your dreams, but to believe God—the One who created you and your dreams. Surrounding yourself with people who believe in you is wonderful, but building your hope solely on human encouragement is not enough. Not everyone will believe you, and there will be people who try to shut you down. I still encounter people who don't take me seriously, but now I have a trust and security in God that is greater than their opinions. I trust that God created me exactly for this moment and exactly for this job, to be the best mom, wife, pastor, speaker, and author that I can possibly be. The same is true for you. God created us, and He hasn't asked us to give our level best without giving His level best to help us succeed. He takes us seriously, and that's why we can put our hope and trust in Him.

We not only have to trust Him more than others; we have to trust Him more than ourselves. I know well that sometimes the most discouraging critic you'll face is the one you see in the mirror every day. Whether your past hurts were from mistakes you made, what someone did to you, or a loss you had no control over, somewhere down the line,

I'm sure you've had some of those self-loathing thoughts float through your head—that it was all your fault, and that you can't dream again because you can't trust yourself. When such thoughts arise, I encourage you to take your quiet time before God and ask Him to tell you who you are and what you're capable of. Let Him remind you of His promises over your life. Let the God of hope fill you with hope, as Paul prayed: "I pray that God, the source of hope, will fill you completely with joy and peace because you trust in him. Then you will overflow with confident hope through the power of the Holy Spirit" (Romans 15:13).

Chapter 5

OUT OF THE DEPTHS

---

*"Share each other's burdens,
and in this way obey the law of Christ."*

GALATIANS 6:2

Elisabeth Kübler-Ross, the Swiss-American psychologist who developed the theory of the five stages of grief, wrote, "The most beautiful people we have known are those who have known defeat, known suffering, known struggle, known loss, and have found their way out of the depths. These persons have an appreciation, a sensitivity, and an understanding of life that fills them with compassion, gentleness, and a deep loving concern. Beautiful people do not just happen."[4]

There's nothing magical about suffering and loss that cause them to make us better people. Countless people around the world have suffered and never "found their way out of the depths." But it's equally

---

[4] Elisabeth Kübler-Ross, *Death: The Final Stage of Growth* (New York: Touchstone, 1986), 96.

true that every person who has developed the capacity for great compassion has done so through the experience of suffering—either their own suffering, or that of those they have loved.

The difference between those who remain lost in the "depths" and those who find their way out is largely determined by how they answer this question: "Will I allow this loss, failure, struggle, or pain to cause me to turn my focus inward on myself and move away from others, or will I choose to focus outward and move towards others?" Only those who choose, in the face of suffering, to look *up* to God and *out* to others and reach out for connection are those who ultimately gain this beautiful, Christ-like capacity of compassion.

As I mentioned in Chapter 1, the word *compassion* comes from Latin roots that mean "to suffer with." Dictionary.com defines the word as "a feeling of deep sympathy and sorrow for another who is stricken by misfortune, accompanied by a strong desire to alleviate the suffering." Compassion is the ability to step into someone else's pain or struggle and carry it with them. Becoming a compassionate person is one of the greatest things we can learn in life, and is the ultimate sign of true friendship and Christ-like character.

DON'T WANT PITY

Compassion is a capacity we must develop and a skill we must learn. None of us knows merely by instinct how to move towards someone who is hurting and offer help. Perhaps one of the greatest ways we develop the skill of compassion is by experiencing the different ways people respond to us when we are hurting. When you're in the midst of pain, it becomes crystal clear which kinds of responses bring comfort and relief, and which don't.

When I was in the "depths" after losing Jet, it was quite eye-opening to discover who among the people around me knew how to move towards someone in pain and who really didn't. Some people simply retreated from me, apparently unsure of what to say or do. Others offered their condolences and told me they were sorry for my loss, yet somehow their approach put me at arm's length, as if to say, "I really don't want to feel your pain." Still others, as I mentioned in Chapter 2, tried to find a silver lining in my loss that wasn't a silver lining at all: "It could have been worse. At least it wasn't one of your daughters!" It staggered me that people thought it would be comforting to insinuate that my son's life was somehow worth less than my daughters' lives. At least now I know firsthand that offering people fake silver linings is not an expression of compassion!

Then there were the people who "got it." Instead of standing back from my pain in silence, or throwing out meaningless platitudes—"Bummer for you, but look on the bright side!"—these people showed true compassion and empathy. They joined me in the "depths." They sat and listened to me process my pain, sometimes for hours. They hugged me and cried with me. They *asked* me how they could be there for me instead of assuming or guessing. Everything they did sent the message that my pain mattered, and that they wanted to help me carry it.

I don't know about you, but I don't enjoy being on the receiving end of pity. Pity is annoying. The posture of pity says, "I feel bad for you, but not enough to actually help. So I'm just going to say something that sounds compassionate without really showing compassion." Pity watches the journey, and ultimately leaves you alone in your pain. In contrast, compassion joins you in your pain, carries hope through the journey, and in doing so, empowers you to move through the pain and into recovery.

If you want to give hope to a person in pain, then the best thing to do is just to be with them in their pain. Give them the permission and strength to feel *with you* what they are unable to feel alone because it's too frightening, crushing, and overwhelming. Support them by being able to listen, even if they keep rehashing the same event and repeating the same thoughts and feelings. Sometimes the verbal process of a hurting person provides a lot of healing. Let them cry on your shoulder. Comfort them by letting them know that you're on their side. This is how you share their burden, and give them strength to carry it out of the depths.

TRUE FRIENDSHIP

Suffering *with* someone is an act of connection—an act of friendship. There's nothing like suffering to show you who your true friends are, and to make your true friends even truer. The connection I have with those who shared my pain and showed me compassion in my grieving process is far deeper than before I entered it, and I am deeply grateful for these friendships.

However, the contrasting experiences of receiving both compassion and pity in the midst of suffering has brought clarity and passion to who *I* want to be as a friend to others. Simply put, I don't want to be one of those "fair weather" friends who can only offer pity when someone I love is hurting. I want to be a true friend who moves towards them with compassion and empathy. I want to brave the "depths" and help them come out on the other side, strengthened, healed, and whole.

There are many examples of compassionate friendship in the Bible, but one I find especially impressive is Jonathan's friendship with David. Scripture tells us that these two men hit it off right away:

> *After David had finished talking with Saul, he met Jonathan, the king's son. There was an immediate bond between them, for Jonathan loved David. From that day on Saul kept David with him and wouldn't let him return home. And Jonathan made a solemn pact with David, because he loved him as he loved himself. Jonathan sealed the pact by taking off his robe and giving it to David, together with his tunic, sword, bow, and belt.*
> (1 Samuel 18:1-4)

Notice, it was Jonathan who loved David first. He initiated a covenant friendship with David, and essentially elevated him to be equal with his own princely status by giving him his personal garments and weapons. Everyone who witnessed Jonathan giving David this highly admirable gift would have understood that Jonathan, the heir to the throne, was committing his honor and possessions to serve David. It's stunning that right from the start of their relationship, Jonathan wasn't envious or jealous of David, but instead offered to serve David and honor his call to be the next king of Israel.

Jonathan's loyalty and love for David proved even more genuine when Jonathan's own father, Saul, fell prey to jealousy and envy upon seeing David's growing popularity and tried to have him assassinated. Jonathan hid David from Saul and got him to safety. Then, some time later, as Saul's manhunt for David continued, Jonathan sought David out and encouraged him:

> *Jonathan went to find David and encouraged him to stay strong in his faith in God. "Don't be afraid," Jonathan reassured him. "My father will never find you! You are going to be the king of Israel, and I will be next to you, as my father, Saul, is well aware." So the two of them renewed their solemn pact before the LORD. Then Jonathan returned home, while David stayed at Horesh.*
> (1 Samuel 23:16-18)

The NIV says, "Jonathan...helped [David] find his strength in the Lord." Wow! What an amazing contrast between two men, a father and son, who both recognized the favor and call on David's life. Saul, the father, felt threatened by David and tried to kill him. But Jonathan, the son, who could have felt just as threatened by the fact that David would take the throne instead of him, only ever moved toward him as a friend—a true friend. Jonathan reminded David of who he was, encouraged him in his calling, and helped him find strength in the Lord. He ministered to David and served him. In my experience, there's no more incredible way to love a friend than to protect them, serve them, and encourage them in their calling!

David's son, Solomon, wrote, "A man of many companions may come to ruin, but there is a friend who sticks closer than a brother" (Proverbs 18:24). I can only imagine that David, in passing his wisdom on to Solomon, told him about his first true friend, Jonathan, and how he never would have become king without Jonathan's loyalty, protection, and encouragement. Jonathan was a friend who stuck closer than a brother.

Another powerful example of compassionate friendship in the Bible is found in the book of Mark:

> They gathered in such large numbers that there was no room left, not even outside the door, and [Jesus] preached the word to them. Some men came, bringing to him a paralyzed man, carried by four of them. Since they could not get him to Jesus because of the crowd, they made an opening in the roof above Jesus by digging through it and then lowered the mat the man was lying on. When Jesus saw their faith, he said to the paralyzed man, "Son, your sins are forgiven." (Mark 2:2-5)

This paralyzed man had nothing left. He was utterly powerless to do anything for himself. It seems he didn't even have faith to be healed. The passage says that it was when Jesus saw *"their faith"*—the friends' faith—that He first forgave the man of his sins, and a few verses later, told the man to take up his mat and walk. Jesus acknowledged that this man's friends had faith for him when he couldn't fight the fight any longer. They were willing to sacrifice the time and effort to carry their friend through town to the house where Jesus was and dig through a roof with their bare hands, sweating in the heat. They then refused to leave their friend until they saw his miracle.

I love this picture! I want to be that kind of friend. I don't want to be the person who just says, "Wow, what a bummer that you're paralyzed." I want to say, "I'll sacrifice my time and energy to see you set free and become who you're called to be!"

MOVING TOWARDS

We all have people around us who are hurting. In some cases, the hurt is big and obvious. Divorce, illness, death, or some other tragedy has touched their lives, and they are suffering grief, pain, and loss. In other cases, the hurt is hidden or seemingly small. No matter what it is, our calling as members of the same spiritual family is the same: "Share each other's burdens, and in this way obey the law of Christ" (Galatians 6:2).

Sometimes it's actually easier for us to move toward and rally around someone with a big, obvious burden like cancer, because it's not hard to feel deep compassion for them. It's harder to feel and show compassion when your friend comes to you with a burden that, from your perspective, doesn't seem like that big of a deal. When a friend, for example, tells you that they're having a bad day because of something that appears ridiculous compared to whatever you're going through, it can be tempting to step back and make a judgment about their suffering, rather than moving towards them.

The first thing to do in these moments is remind yourself that it's impossible to compare one person's sufferings with another. Nowhere in the Bible does it say that one person's pain is more important than another's. Instead, it says that God shows no favoritism (see Acts 10:34). Jesus cared just as much about saving the host of a wedding from the embarrassment of running out of wine as he cared about raising His friend Lazarus from death. He cares about everything relating to matters of the heart.

None of us knows what it actually feels like to carry the burden another person carrying. All we need to know is that we're supposed to help each other carry our burdens, whatever they may be. The fact that another person's burden seems light to you may be a sign that you have grace on your life to help them carry it. Conversely, the burdens that seem impossibly heavy to you may seem light to someone else, who can therefore offer their strength to help you. If we refuse to make judgments and commit to moving toward our brothers and sisters with compassion, no matter what, then the grace of Jesus will enable us to carry loads together that none of us can carry alone.

After refusing to step away from a friend or judge their situation, the next step is to move toward their situation and try to understand it better. This is the skill of empathy. Empathy is feeling *with* someone; it's putting yourself in their shoes. It's using your imagination to share and understand their experience, which then sets you up to understand what they need and how you can truly help them in their situation. Empathy is essential to compassion and connection with other people.

When we move toward one another with empathy and compassion, we are imitating Christ Himself, who has carried every burden for us, no matter how big or small. Jesus is our truest, best Friend, who sacrificed everything not only to suffer *with* us, but also to suffer *for* us. He went to the depth of depths—to hell itself—and came out on the other side as the most beautiful, perfect model of compassion. He always moves toward us in our suffering, always shares our pain, and always will use it to make us into compassionate, beautiful friends like Him. There is no greater gift we have received than His friendship, and no greater gift we can give than to be that kind of true friend to others.

Chapter 6

STRONG AS DEATH

Place me like a seal over your heart,
like a seal on your arm.
For love is as strong as death,
its jealousy as enduring as the grave.
Love flashes like fire,
the brightest kind of flame.
Many waters cannot quench love,
nor can rivers drown it.

SONG OF SONGS 8:6-7A

I still remember how my voice trembled with conviction as I said my marriage vows. With the words, "In sickness and in health...in good times and in bad," I wholly committed my heart and life to love Chris forever, no matter what trials came our way.

Admittedly, it was hard to comprehend what "sickness" and "bad times" really meant on our wedding day, given that we were both in good health and blissfully in love. The biggest challenge before us was figuring out how to pay our bills. Before long, we had that down, and moved confidently forward in tackling what turned out to be a pretty standard lineup of marriage adventures—buying our first house, finding out we were going to be parents, juggling work and home schedules, adding baby #2, moving, and keeping our connection strong in all the busyness and chaos.

I still remember how my voice trembled with conviction as I said my marriage vows. With the words, "In sickness and in health...in good times and in bad," I wholly committed my heart and life to love Chris forever, no matter what trials came our way.

Admittedly, it was hard to comprehend what "sickness" and "bad times" really meant on our wedding day, given that we were both in good health and blissfully in love. The biggest challenge before us was figuring out how to pay our bills. Before long, we had that down, and moved confidently forward in tackling what turned out to be a pretty standard lineup of marriage adventures—buying our first house, finding out we were going to be parents, juggling work and home schedules, adding baby #2, moving, and keeping our connection strong in all the busyness and chaos.

Then the "bad time" came. Will we ever have to face something more devastating than the loss of a child? After walking through it, it's difficult for me to imagine that we will, though of course, there is no way of knowing. All I know is that losing Jet required Chris and me to fulfill our vow to love each other as we never had before.

SHUT DOWN, NOT SHUT OUT

There's really no way to prepare for that first big test in marriage, the event that brings one or both of you to your limits and reveals what you'll do when you get there. Will you hold on through the storm, or fall apart? Will you move towards one another, or retreat and put up walls around your pain? How will you respond when you see what the test exposes in the person you love?

For Chris and me, the first experience of reaching our limits took place in the hospital the day Jet was born. Shortly after they induced me, I decided I wanted an epidural. Having given birth to my two daughters with no drugs, I knew the pain that was coming, and I suddenly realized that on top of all the trauma and emotional pain, I couldn't handle any more.

Chris fully supported this decision and held me through the contractions until the anesthesiologist arrived. By that point, I was more than ready to feel nothing but blessed numbness taking over half of my body. When the anesthesiologist inserted the needle in my back, however, something strange happened. It felt like a camera flash popped right in front of my eyes—for a moment I couldn't see anything, then only streaks of light. These effects quickly subsided however, so I brushed it off and hoped that whatever had happened wasn't serious. I lay back flat on the bed and waited for the drugs to do their job.

Twenty minutes later, I began to feel intense pressure at the back of my skull. The flashing lights reappeared in my field of vision, and my ears started pulsing strangely. In agony, I asked Chris to turn off every light in the room. Through the fog of pain, I heard Chris calling the nurse and explaining that I had a bad headache.

"It's probably due to shock and trauma," she said. "Sometimes the body shuts down in denial when experiencing a loss like this. We'll get her something to help the pain."

Never before had I been so completely incapacitated. It was quite simply the worst pain I had ever felt in my life. Though the fentanyl they administered through my IV helped to diminish the pressure in my head somewhat, I remained unable to open my eyes or move my head. I don't know how long I lay there, unmoving, but eventually I heard the nurse's voice through the haze telling me it was time to push. I took everything in me to gather my wits and obey her. After I managed two short pushes, they told me I could stop. Moments later, the nurse laid Jet's tiny body in my arms.

I wanted to hold him forever, but within minutes, it seemed, the fentanyl had begun to wear off and the pressure in my head returned with vengeance. A wave of nausea overtook me, and I just had time to hand Jet over to Chris before vomiting. Unable to speak or open my eyes, I lay back on the bed, delirious with pain and slipping towards unconsciousness. The last thing I heard before I fell asleep was someone in the room asking, "What's wrong with her?" and the nurse explaining again that I was suffering from shock and trauma.

I slept through the night and awoke with what felt like a normal migraine headache. I was still sensitive to light, nauseous, and exhausted, but I could finally function again. I sat up and saw Jethro's body lying in a crib next to the bed. Apparently he had been beside me all night. I immediately rushed to hold him. I was devastated to learn that I had missed his first bath and lost seven precious hours of time with him, apparently because I had been so shut down by grief and trauma. Distraught, I apologized repeatedly to my cold son and my heartbroken husband, who had spent the night holding everything together for me. Despite all his assurances and words of comfort, all I could feel as we said our final goodbyes to Jet and drove home was guilt for being so emotionally distant and out of it.

Then around 2 a.m. the next night, I woke up with that same excruciating pain in my head and frantically stumbled to the bathroom to throw up. This time, I knew something was very wrong, and I was sure it wasn't shock, guilt, or anxiety. I couldn't bring myself to wake Chris, however, so I went back to bed and slept fitfully till he woke up around 7 a.m. Weakly, I explained to him what had happened during the night and he agreed that we needed to go back to the ER.

When I described my symptoms at the ER, the doctor immediately diagnosed me with a *spinal headache*. If an epidural is not done in exactly the right place (and even the best anesthesiologist won't do it perfectly 100% of the time), he explained, it can cause spinal fluid to leak and throw off the pressure balance of fluid around the spinal cord and brain, causing intense pain. He then told me that in order to stop the leak, I needed a *blood patch*. The procedure was simple—he would draw blood from my arm and inject it into my spine at the site where the epidural was done—but it would take a few hours to complete, and I would need to lie completely still the entire time.

Have you ever been forced to be still somewhere when everything in you wants to run out of there screaming? With every minute of lying in that hospital room and doing my utmost to stay motionless, I grew more and more angry that I was there. Why couldn't I be home grieving with my girls? Why did I have to be back in this place where we had suffered so much, where we had just parted from the body of our son? I never wanted to be in a hospital again, yet there I was less than twenty-four hours later, listening to the nursery rhyme music that played through the hospital speakers whenever a baby was born. It felt like a cruel joke—not only was I being forced to remember the nightmare of the last two days; the injustice of it was being rubbed in my face.

Yet even as the storm of anger, grief, anxiety, guilt, and pain raged inside, more positive thoughts and feelings began to filter into my awareness. For one thing, I now knew the reason I had shut down so completely the day before. I hadn't been having some kind of traumatic emotional breakdown at all—I had been physically injured! It was such a relief to know that I wasn't going crazy.

For another, I began to appreciate the fact that Chris, who had also believed my irrational behavior was due to grief and trauma, had never once reacted with the slightest bit of frustration or disappointment. I knew my shutting down must have felt like I was shutting him out. I knew it must have been difficult for the responsibility of making all the funeral arrangements to fall on him while I lay there, totally unresponsive. I knew it had been distressing to have me hand Jet over to him and then throw up, as though I couldn't handle the sight of his body. And I knew he had been sad that I couldn't be present and able to share those hours with Jet together. Yet he had stood beside me the whole time, steadily offering his strength, love, and support.

In those moments, I came face to face with the reality of true human love. I felt as though I was getting to see that even if I had been willfully *choosing* to shut down, Chris would have responded the same way. He would have stayed beside me, just as he was there with me again in the ER. I knew it was as awful for him to be back in the hospital as it was for me, yet as I lay there fuming, he was gently wiping my forehead and comforting me in my pain. Chris held my hand for the entire blood patch procedure, refusing to leave my side even for a bathroom break. How could I not fall in love with my husband even more?

Along with the gift of my husband's love, God gave us a gift that brought so much comfort and relief to my ragged heart. The day after I received the blood patch, I mercifully woke up without a headache. However, waves of anger continued to course through me as I began to face the reality of loss. It kept hitting me that I would never stare at Jet's adorable chin again, or feel his precious lips against mine. I could barely remember what he had looked like and only had a few pictures of him taken by my family. Why didn't God protect my son from death? On top of that, why didn't He at least protect me from the wrongly administered epidural that stole precious time away from holding my boy? Why couldn't just *one* thing have gone right?

We had a few remaining details to arrange with the funeral home that day, so Chris made the call. I could physically feel the pain choking his voice as he answered the funeral director's questions about Jet's cremation. Then, just before he hung up, Chris asked, "Where is our son now?" An image of a cold, sterile, metal drawer in a morgue flashed in my mind. Then I heard, "Can we come see him?"

I whipped my head up to look at Chris, instantly on the edge of my seat. See him? I didn't even know that was an option!

An hour later, we were in a private, peaceful, warm room looking down at our son, who lay wrapped in a white sheet on a pillow as though he was simply taking a nap. We spent over an hour there crying, taking turns snuggling him, and memorizing each detail of his precious and perfectly formed body. We wrapped him in a blanket that our oldest daughter had picked out for him, and showed him some of the superhero posters that had decorated the walls of his waiting nursery. God restored that invaluable time to my heartbroken mother's heart, and I will forever be grateful for that hour we had to make memories of each of his features.

TAKING THE WAVES

After surviving those days of trauma in the hospital, Chris and I reaffirmed our commitment that no matter what we were in, we were in it together. Even when we seemed shut down, we would never shut one another out. As we began to walk out the journey of grieving, we soon discovered just how important this commitment was. It turns out that two people can grieve the same loss, yet have entirely different experiences of grief. Chris's relationship with Jet was different than mine, so the loss meant different things to him. Our pain was at different levels on different days. Some days, he would be feeling pain and confusion just as I was feeling that the pain was more manageable and I could finally come up for a breath of air. Navigating how to love each other through the emotional ups and downs was challenging.

Initially, we were both at a loss to figure out how we could help one another through the pain in the moments when we could barely manage our own. The first few weeks after losing Jet were particularly difficult because they fell during the Christmas holidays. Chris and I both felt constrained in processing our grief because we had family visiting and we wanted our girls to be able to enjoy their cousins and all the festivities. We did our best to handle our emotions privately. I mostly zoned out on the couch watching Disney Channel movies while the kids played with their cousins. Meanwhile, Chris distracted himself by playing video games with his brother-in-law.

One afternoon, the kids were playing in the backyard while I stared blankly at one of my cheesy Disney movies, trying not to let myself think. I could hear Chris and my brother-in-law in Chris's office talking about fighter planes and missiles. Out of nowhere, a wave of pain and anger that I was having a Christmas without one of my children washed over me. I stood up and walked into the office, gave my husband a look that said I needed him, and he immediately followed me up to our bedroom. Without a word, I collapsed on the bed in tears. Chris just held me until I got it all out and was able to pull myself back together.

Later that night, I saw Chris staring off into nothing at the dinner table as our relatives laughed and shared Christmas leftovers. Soon, he quietly left the room and snuck upstairs to our bedroom. I knew he was in a rough spot, but I didn't get up to join him right away. I had felt better since my afternoon crying session, and I wanted that feeling to last. I just didn't feel like I could handle falling apart again. So I selfishly told myself he was okay, and watched my girls giggle as they played with their Christmas presents.

After about fifteen minutes, however, I couldn't take it anymore. Chris had come right away when I needed him earlier, and I had to do the same. As I climbed the stairs, I took a deep breath and braced myself to do what I had to do as a wife and lover, to love him through his pain even when I felt raw myself. I was terrified as he cried beside me while I ran my fingers through his curly hair. I wanted so much to be strong, to find the perfect words to comfort him, but everything sounded wrong in my head. As the moments lengthened, however, I realized that just being there for him was the best thing I could do for him, just as he had done for me. Neither of us needed words; we simply needed to cry healing tears that would release the pain. And being in one another's presence somehow made the tears flow more easily.

After that day, Chris and I learned to let ourselves cry through the tidal waves of pain that hit each of us at different times. We learned to be there for another in those moments, but to leave space for each of us to express and work through our thoughts and emotions as we needed. We learned not to take one another's pain personally. We learned to appreciate our unique grieving processes. As we did so, we felt more connected and more healed. The tidal waves came less and less frequently.

And then one day, I noticed that the tidal waves felt different—or more specifically, I discovered that I could choose to feel them differently. Instead of feeling them as waves of pain, I could choose to feel them as waves of love—love for a boy I carried for nine months, love for his father, our marriage, and our other beautiful children, and love for the God who brought all of us together and continues to overwhelm us with His comfort and safety.

Though the waves still come at times, I no longer dread the tears. I welcome them. Every time, they remind me that I am not alone in my pain. I am fully loved and held by a man who has never left my side, and never will, for as long as we both shall live. Through the faithfulness and grace of the One who made us one, we will always face our tomorrows together.

Chapter 7

TATTOOED BY GOODNESS

But thank God! He has made us his captives and continues to lead us along in Christ's triumphal procession. Now he uses us to spread the knowledge of Christ everywhere, like a sweet perfume.

2 CORINTHIANS 2:14

Growing up, I was taught that Jesus called His followers to be "salt" and "light" in the world (see Matthew 5:13-14). This meant that we were not to retreat from the world around us, but were to influence it for good. For a long time, whenever I heard this teaching I found myself asking, "But how can my little life have influence?" Like many of us, I used to associate influence with things that are big and public—politicians, entertainers, CEOs, the government, the economy, the culture. Being none of these, I assumed that there was little I could do to impact the world around me in any significant way.

Then I learned that big, visible things are not the only sources of influence. Because we live in a world where everyone is connected, everyone has influence. Even the smallest, most obscure people can affect the whole, just as tiny germ can make your whole body sick and equally tiny antibodies can make you well again. In fact, when we trace any particular innovation or movement that caused a significant shift in society and culture back to its beginnings, from technology to fashion to spiritual revival, we find that it was usually started in obscurity by just a few people. The story of the gospel itself is a story about people who were all but invisible to the famous and powerful of the day. If anything proves that big change comes from small change, it's the story of Christ and His Church carrying His gospel into the world.

Funnily enough, parenting has impressed on me how even the smallest person can influence the world around them. In our family's little kingdom, every one of us affects the whole—including our youngest daughter, Aria. Every time precious Aria opens her mouth, it affects our environment. Aria has absolutely no concept of an "inside voice." Everything, from simple observations to questions, giggles, or tantrums, comes out of her mouth at the same volume: LOUD. We have no idea where her extreme loudness comes from. We tried everything to get her learn how to quiet down and finally realized we were fighting a losing battle. The only thing we could do was let her be herself.

As we have allowed Aria's influence to be felt in our environment, I have come to believe that Aria's extreme loudness is one of her gifts to the world. She attracts attention because of her volume, and keeps it because she's sweet and funny, even in her loudness. Whenever we're in a group, heads turn when they hear my daughter shouting something like, "MOMMA, WHERE WE GOIN'!?" at the top of her voice. Instead of seeing her on the verge of a meltdown, as they might expect, they find her face full of excitement and joy, and can't help smiling themselves. I love to picture her as an old woman, eyes bright with laughter, and enjoying a house full of loud music and friends and family. Aria is the epitome of a good time.

I understand that my job as Aria's mother is not to limit her influence, but to teach her how to use it wisely. And that is the job facing each of us. We all have influence, wherever we live and work, whatever our socioeconomic status, or whatever our gifts and talents. We should not be asking, "How can I have influence?" but "Who am I called to influence, and how am I called to influence them?"

THE GOODNESS OF GOD

God will answer the "who" question differently for each of us, but the answer to the "how" question with have a common thread for all of us. No matter who God calls us to influence, and no matter what vehicle He has given us for influence, the substance of that influence is *good news*—the news of how He is restoring our lives and revealing His love as we walk in relationship with Him. But this good news will only impact others to the degree that it has impacted us. It's our transformation, not our information, that offers people something that can change them. If we hope to show others the good news of the gospel, then it has to come from our own stories of encountering and being changed by the goodness of God.

My husband and I now have a story of encountering God's goodness throughout the experience of losing a child. I may not fully understand why my son isn't here, or why other children die every of cancer and other causes. But I fully understand that through it all, God has been and will be there. He promises His peace and assurance, and I have seen the fruit of those promises. Since this is something I fully understand, I can influence anyone who crosses my path and needs to hear it.

Two months after we lost Jet, Chris and I decided to get tattoos in his memory.[5] We felt these tattoos

---

[5] I realize tattoos are a touchy subject for Christians who hold that they fall into the category prohibited by Leviticus: "Ye shall not make any cuttings in your flesh for the dead, nor print any marks upon you: I *am* the LORD" (Leviticus 19:28 KJV). Other Christians, including Chris and me, feel it is a gray area, seeing as this verse is referring specifically to pagan rituals that are far removed from most tattooing in our culture.

would serve to remind us that Jet's short little life was a testimony of God's goodness in our lives—and be a vehicle for us to share that testimony with others. Chris and I could think of no better way to do this than to make his name visible for anyone to see. We agreed have the tattoos placed on our outer left forearms, and pored over fonts until we each picked out our favorite.

Nearly every single week since getting our tattoos, someone has stopped and asked me what my tattoo says. It simply says, "Jethro Dylan," but the script I chose is swirly and not easy to read. Each time, the question has opened a door for me to briefly tell our story, which I always finish by saying, "Our son was a gift, and I'm so thankful that God provided a safe place in heaven for him to wait for me!"

Quite a few of the people I have talked to seem surprised to hear that I'm not bitter or angry towards God over losing Jet. Many Christians, I have found, struggle with feeling anger towards God in the face of losing a loved one, blame Him for not intervening, or even accuse Him of taking the person away Himself. When I have explained that God didn't take my son, some people have given me incredulous looks. In a few of those instances, I have gone on to share that the enemy is the one who comes to kill, steal, and destroy, not God. God is the One who has defeated death through Christ and is mercifully redeeming all things, even though we still feel the pangs of death and loss in this life. It saddens me that believers would fall for such lies about God's character, and thus push Him, the supreme Comforter, away from them in the midst of grief and loss. I'm thankful for each time my tattoo has opened a conversation in which I can remind Christians of His goodness and urge them to seek Him in their pain.

Many other people who have asked about my tattoo are not believers, and I've found that telling them my story is one of the easiest ways to introduce them to a good God. One of these beautiful encounters took place at a nail salon shortly after I got my tattoo. A friend told me I needed to relax and be spoiled, and gave me a gift card to get a manicure and pedicure. I didn't argue with her, and made an appointment at the salon right away.

It so happened that I had visited that particular salon a few times during my pregnancy with Jet. When I walked through the door for my appointment, I was really hoping no one would remember me so I could just enjoy some pampering and not talk to anyone. I sat down in a spa chair, used the remote to turn on the massage, sank my feet into the warm, bubbling water, and closed my eyes. The blissful moment evaporated, however, when the nail esthetician came over to me.

"Oh, hi!" she said, smiling broadly in recognition. "You had your baby! Let me see pictures of him! You said his name was going to be Jeff...or maybe Judd?"

Immediately, my eyes filled with tears. I really did not want to talk about what had happened. Saying the words out loud felt like daggers piercing my chest. My throat closed up and my heart started racing. I opened my mouth to speak, bracing myself for the oncoming, full-on breakdown that seemed inevitable. The only thing I could say was, "He's in heaven. He's not here."

She looked at me in confusion. Then suddenly, the meaning of my words dawned on her—my son was dead, not alive, and there was no celebrating to be done.

"I'm so sorry," she mumbled. Without another word, she busied herself with trimming my toenails and scrubbing the dead skin off my heels.

I leaned back, closed my eyes, and allowed the relief of silence to envelop me as I attempted to stem the tide of painful memories. I began to enter a daydream I had often had since losing Jet—a blurry but glorious picture of my boy in heaven with a smile on his face. As soon as I saw this picture, I felt that I needed to tell the nail esthetician that I was not only living in a story of sadness, but also a story of hope. I opened my eyes and was just about to say something about my son when she beat me to it.

"You got a tattoo," she observed. "What does it say?" She had a cautious, tentative look in her eyes, apparently hoping it was a safe subject to bring up.

I smiled brightly and said, "Yeah, it's my son's name. Jethro Dylan. He's a beautiful boy. I actually do have some pictures if you want to see them."

Still looking cautious, she nodded politely. As I took out my phone and scrolled through some of the photos of my sweet boy, I told her about the beauty of his labor. I told her that the entire time, I felt sadness that he was gone, but also complete peace in knowing where he was. I told her that I was so thankful for heaven and for a God who opened His arms to hold my newborn's spirit, even as I briefly held his body. I explained that while I missed him so much, I felt grateful knowing that one of my children would never have tears or aches or scraped knees or broken hearts or financial difficulties. One of my children only knows a completely blissful life, I said, and he's waiting for me—a long wait for me, but a short wait for him! I could ask for no better outcome than having a happy little boy.

As the nail esthetician listened, tears welled in her eyes, and she couldn't help giving me a small smile. After I had finished describing my perspective, she said quietly, "I wish I knew your God. You make it sound like a fairy tale. I've never heard anyone describe heaven like that."

"What god do you know?" I asked, interested.

"I don't know or believe in any gods. But I have to say that for the first time in my life I'm actually curious about the God of the Bible."

I then invited her to come to my church. She thanked me, but said she was moving out of state the next week. When I left, I initially felt disappointed that I hadn't been able to lead her into a relationship with Jesus. But then I realized I had led her *toward* one. I didn't need to be the one to pray a sinner's prayer with her or bring her to church for the first time. All I needed to do was plant a seed in her heart by honestly portraying the God I serve. She definitely seemed open to Him after our conversation. Though the next steps were out of my hands, I could rest in peace knowing that our family's story is nestled somewhere in her brain. She'll always remember that crazy lady who talked about a God who was good and beautiful, like a fairy tale.

HIS GOODNESS IS REAL

One of the best signs that we are showing people the real God is that they begin to see how He can be good—almost too good to be true—in the midst of this world of pain, suffering, and sin. So many people in the world reject the idea of God because they can't imagine how a good God would allow such things. It's our privilege to show them how God's goodness is at work in these realities, bringing healing, restoration, redemption, and joy.

God's goodness in our lives has the power to influence others because it is real and attractive. Unfortunately, it seems like a lot of Christians think that the way to influence the world is not with God's goodness, but with fear and intimidation. Scripture tells us that it is God's goodness that leads us to repentance (see Romans 2:4), and that His love is to be our motive for calling people to Christ: "Christ's love controls us," Paul wrote, "...For God was in Christ, reconciling the world to himself, no longer counting people's sins against them. And he gave us this wonderful message of reconciliation" (2 Corinthians 4:14, 19).

The people around us are starving for something real and authentic, but they have no idea where to find it. Everyone loves it when someone decides to bare all and "tell their story," because somewhere in there people hope to find a raw truth that can feed their spiritual hunger for reality. But there's only one source of truth and reality, and this is what we as Christians have to offer in our stories. Our stories are authentic and life-giving—not because we are willing to share all our secrets publicly, but because they are stories of the goodness of God.

For my part, I want my faith in the goodness of God to be loud, just like my daughter Aria's voice. I want people to turn their heads, wondering why I'm so happy, and I want to be able to show them the consistency of God's goodness—now and anywhere! It's a joy and privilege to be able to stand up and say, "Here is where you find reality. God is good, He loves you, and I have proof in my own life."

Chapter 8

CLOSER STILL
BY CHRIS QUILALA

My whole life has been dedicated to ministering to Jesus in worship and leading others to do the same. Since I was a teenager, there has hardly been a week when I was not leading or playing in a worship band, writing worship songs, working on a worship album, traveling to lead worship somewhere, or pastoring other worship leaders. Day after day, I sing lyrics declaring who God is and giving praise and honor to Him for His goodness, faithfulness, kindness, power, and love. I get to live in the joy of His presence and stay in awe of how He shows up when His people pour out their hearts to Him. Honestly, I can't think of any other way I'd rather spend my time. While it's true that everything we do in life can be offered to God as an act of worship, my favorite place to meet Him is in songs of adoration and praise. The idea that this will be one of our main activities in heaven makes me really happy.

Of all the worship sessions I've participated in, however, there has never been one quite like the one Alyssa and I hosted with our family and friends in our living room, and later in the hospital, after learning that our son, Jethro, had no heartbeat.

In those hours, I had to hold together three truths that stretched my soul beyond anything I had ever experienced. The first truth was that my son, according to medical experts, technology, and all other physical evidence, was no longer alive. The second truth was that God could raise the dead. And the third truth was that no matter the outcome, God was still good, sovereign, and worthy of worship.

None of these truths was really in question for me. The doctor's conclusion after the sonogram, devastating as it was to hear, was undeniable. We were in no doubt that only a miracle could reverse it. Yet even though my heart already felt heavy with grief and hopelessness, I knew we would pray for that miracle. Having grown up in a church and movement where I was constantly exposed to the overwhelming evidence in Scripture, history, countless testimonies, and my own experience that God is a miracle-working God, I carried a core value that we were to expect Him to show up in impossible circumstances.

The presence of our pastor, Bill Johnson, made it much easier to press in for a miracle, because Bill had long been my model for how to pray in these kinds of situations. Nine years earlier, I had the amazing honor of standing with our community alongside

Bill and the whole Johnson family as they prayed for Bill's father, Earl, who was fighting terminal cancer. It was powerful to watch Bill grieving, yet never wavering in the truths he had always preached and practiced—that Jesus paid for our healing on the cross, and that He called us to walk in His anointing and authority over sin, sickness, and death. It was even more powerful to experience the way Bill led our community to respond when Earl went to be with the Lord. He simply announced that we must not let an outcome we didn't understand shake our trust in what we did know—God's character and will revealed in the Word and in our lives. We wouldn't let the lack of a specific miracle in one situation shut down our awareness and gratitude for all the other miracles God has done and is doing. Faith that pleases God, Bill reminded us, lies in holding on to eternal, invisible reality in the tension of ever-changing temporal, visible reality. So even as we grieve the loss of those we love or feel disappointed by a certain outcome, we must not allow that grief and disappointment to turn to bitterness and unbelief. We must trust God in the mystery.

Bill also led all of us in worshipping God continuously throughout that entire season of contending for, grieving over, and celebrating the legacy of his father. He explained that the choice to worship God in the midst of loss and disappointment was a precious offering that could only be given to God in those moments. In heaven, sighing and sorrow will end. In eternity, as far as we know, we will never be able to give God the costly sacrifice of praise in the midst of tears. Only in this life, when "weeping may last through the night" (Psalm 30:5), do we have that chance.

Everyone who was part of our community and movement nine years ago remembers Bill's leadership and integrity through that season of loss, and still feels the impact of it. He laid a path for us to follow in any loss or disappointment—a path where we refuse to compromise our faith and trust in God, but choose instead to move closer to Him with confidence and humility.

As Pastor Bill stood in our living room and led us in declaring life over our son, I recognized that this was my chance to take that path myself. This was a moment to demonstrate integrity—to practice not only what my spiritual fathers and mothers had modeled for me, but that which I had myself preached and claimed to believe. For years, I had gotten up day after day, week after week, and sung lyrics like this:

You stay the same through the ages

Your love never changes

There maybe pain in the night but joy comes in the morning

And when the oceans rage

I don't have to be afraid

Because I know that You love me

Your love never fails

Over and over, I had proclaimed that God was the same in every circumstance. If He is unchanging, then my response to Him shouldn't change either. Changing my response in the face of losing my son would mean that I had never actually believed what I had always said about God.

So I worshiped God that night in my living room. I praised Him in the hospital room as my wife labored, and as we held Jethro in our arms and knew there wouldn't be the miracle we had asked and believed for. In the end, more than believing for any particular outcome, we chose to believe in *Him*, and that He was the God we had always believed He was.

BEHIND THE VEIL

A few days after those unforgettable worship sessions, we had another at Jet's memorial service. Each of the songs we chose for the service was a specific declaration we wanted to make to God on that occasion. We sang one of my songs, "My Everything," which says, "You are my Everything, all I need is in You / And all I have, all I am is in You..." We sang Matt Redman's "10,000 Reasons" and declared, "Whatever may pass and whatever lies before me / Let me be singing when the evening comes... / Bless the Lord, oh my soul."[6] And we proclaimed, "In Christ alone my hope is found;

---

[6] Jonas Myrin & Matt Redman, "10,000 Reasons" (Thankyou Music, 2011)

/ He is my light, my strength, my song; / This cornerstone, this solid ground, / Firm through the fiercest drought and storm."[7] Though we had sung these songs hundreds of times, these words seemed so much more powerful and significant because we were consciously paying a price to respond to God out of our pain. We so wanted to give Him what we could only give Him in that moment.

Yet as we reaffirmed who God was to us, and our commitment to Him, the significance of other lines in these songs began to open up to me in new ways. I had always loved the final verses of "10,000 Reasons" and "In Christ Alone," which speak of us entering eternity:

And on that day when my strength is failing

The end draws near and my time has come

Still my soul will sing Your praise unending

10,000 years and then forevermore.[8]

No guilt in life, no fear in death—

This is the pow'r of Christ in me;

From life's first cry to final breath,

Jesus commands my destiny.

No pow'r of hell, no scheme of man,

---

[7] Keith Getty & Stuart Townend, "In Christ Alone" (Kingsway Music, 2001)
[8] "10,000 Reasons"

Can ever pluck me from His hand;
Till He returns or calls me home—
Here in the pow'r of Christ I'll stand.[9]

As I sang these words on this occasion, however, I became overwhelmed as never before with an awareness of eternity. I knew that my son was not dead, but very much alive in the presence of God. Waves of comfort, peace, and longing washed over me as I imagined my boy in the arms of the Father, and knew there would be a day when I would hold him again too.

This awareness of eternity, the sense that the veil between this life and the next is so very thin, has stayed with me since Jet's memorial. I remember the first time I led my song, "Alleluia," after the memorial and sang the words, "With all of heaven we are singing." It seemed as though I could almost hear that sea of voices before the throne, with my son's voice included among them. I feel a connection with heaven now that I never had before. I know heaven is as close as it's ever been, but it feels closer, just because now I know someone who is there.

THE ANCHOR OF THE SOUL

When we enter a grieving process, I know many people can get stuck asking, "Why did You let this

---

[9] "In Christ Alone"

happen, God?" But in the weeks and months that followed Jet's memorial, that question never really came up for me. Instead, I found myself asking, "What now?" I just didn't know what to do with all the ways that losing my son was affecting and rearranging my heart.

The first answer to "What now?" was that I needed to ask that question in a way that moved me towards God rather than away from Him, and that meant being emotionally honest. Sometimes I asked the question in pain and sadness, and other times in intense anger and frustration. But every time, I felt His kindness, goodness, and acceptance wash over me. I experienced the truth that He is a good Father who is not at all scared of my emotions and loves when I am being real and honest with Him.

Sensing His love gave me the next obvious answer to "What now?" and that was to keep doing what I had always done—praising Him. I praised Him for His kindness and mercy, His faithfulness and steadfastness. I praised Him for being the safe place where I could run with my hurt. And without fail, praise brought me back to joy and hope.

Staying in this vulnerable place of honesty and praise before the Lord kept my heart soft, sensitive, and continuing to heal. When we're dealing with emotional pain, it's so easy to start trying to cope by putting up protective walls that shut down our ability to feel. In my case, looking at pictures of my son was a good gauge for me to tell if my heart was starting to become hard or not. There were times when I saw the pictures and instantly started to cry. Other times, I felt anger and frustration and knew I was being tempted to try to protect myself. When that happened, I chose to turn to God and say, "I feel angry and disappointed. But I know You're good and faithful, and I need You." In each of those vulnerable moments, God responded in a way that brought healing and hope to my heart.

The next answer I received to "What now?" was simply to let people know about how we were walking through grieving process and share the hope we were holding on to. Whenever people have asked Alyssa and me if we have struggled with depression since losing Jet, I have been able to tell them honestly that we haven't. While we have both had moments and even days of deep sadness, that sadness has never turned into hopelessness. I know this is because through everything, we have never let go of what we have always known and believed about God. Instead of doubting God and His promises in the face of contrary circumstances, we have done all we can to move towards Him, trust Him, and hold on to Him even more tightly. We have put our hope in Him, and as Hebrews says, this hope has been an anchor for our souls:

> God has given both his promise and his oath.
> These two things are unchangeable because it is
> impossible for God to lie. Therefore, we who have

fled to him for refuge can have great confidence as we hold to the hope that lies before us. This hope is a strong and trustworthy anchor for our souls. (Hebrew 6:18-19)

When believers move away from God in the face of difficult circumstances—and sadly, many of them do—it's a sign that they have not taken hold of Him as their true hope. Hope is an anchor, something solid that cuts through the stormy waves of circumstances and locks us into the immovable reality of God and His promises. His promises are our refuge, our safe place. When we hold on to hope in the face of contrary circumstances, we hold on to the very thing that will make us victorious in those circumstances.

Various people have told me that watching or hearing about how Alyssa and I are choosing to hope in God after losing Jethro has helped them recognize that they have some work to do in the area of faith and hope. My own brother-in-law, who is a Christian, told me he realized he hadn't worked through all the heart effects of losing his mom to cancer some years before. One man came up to me after a meeting and said, "I recently lost a child too." He then admitted it had actually been *nine years* since that loss, which he had allowed to take him down a very dark path. Though he believed in God, he told me, he had never been able to trust God or let the Holy Spirit comfort and heal his heart. Nine years later, he still had walls up and was struggling with bitterness. I prayed that God would give him the grace to drop the walls and open his heart to the amazing kindness and mercy of Jesus.

I definitely have a ton of compassion for people who are trying to trust God in the midst of pain and loss—it's not easy. I know I couldn't have made it through this season in our lives without the strength and example of leaders and friends who have trusted God in loss. They were the ones who taught me that even though trusting God in mystery and disappointment will stretch us to what seems to be the breaking point, it's the only option we can take that won't destroy us. The stretching produces strength, and I count it an honor that I can be one to offer strength I now have to others.

The last answer to "What now?" is that I want to do all I can to sustain and walk in the increased awareness of eternity that I've received now that one of my children is living there. I've always wanted to live my life in the light of eternity, to spend myself so that when I stand before the Lord I hear, "Well done, good and faithful servant." I don't want to build my own kingdom or get caught up caring about things that won't last. But the knowledge that my son is in that realm I'm living for, is in that "cloud of witnesses" that surround me as I run this race, and will be there at the finish line of my life, has made it all more real to me. In everything I do—loving my wife and daughters, ministering to people, and ministering to God—my heart is pointed toward heaven. Every day, I want everything I do to bring me and those around me closer to eternity.

Chapter 9

NEVER DO IT ALONE

Never abandon a friend—either yours or your father's. When disaster strikes, you won't have to ask your brother for assistance. It's better to go to a neighbor than to a brother who lives far away.

PROVERBS 27:10

When I moved to Redding, one of my deep longings was to find people with whom I could build friendships that would last for years to come. Most of the friendships I made growing up were relatively short-lived. My family moved frequently, and technology didn't allow us to be continuously connected as it does now (social media didn't exist, and text messaging had only just arrived on the scene), so relationships usually drifted apart after I drove away. I made one best friend in L.A. with whom I stayed in touch, and we remain close. However, I always held on to the hope that I would finally be in a place where I could cultivate more long-term relationships.

As it turned out, of course, I did meet my life-long best friend in Redding—Chris. But marrying

Chris only deepened my longing for close, lasting friendships. Chris had a very different experience than I had growing up. He was born and raised in Redding, and his best friends were the same ones he had had since preschool! It was a totally new experience for me to hang around Chris's friends and get to know a group of people who had known and loved each other for decades. As Chris told me the stories behind each friendship, it became obvious that each one had weathered highs and lows. They had supported one another through difficult seasons and celebrated milestones, and as a result, they shared a level of deep mutual trust and loyalty. My husband never had to wonder where to go when he needed wisdom, support, help, or even someone to have fun with. He had a relational bank account he had invested in his entire life, which he could draw on whenever he wanted.

Seeing this relational wealth was so attractive to me. I wanted my life and our family's life to be rooted in community like that. I started to dream about my children having the same experience Chris had. I imagined them finding friends with whom they would grow up through elementary, middle, and high school, and maybe even be in each other's weddings and raise children together.

As these hopes and dreams took shape in my heart, I began to be more intentional and focused on building friendships. I considered the women with whom I had connected most in Redding and started asking myself which relationships could go the distance. Who could I see myself connected to for the next ten, twenty, or thirty years? I decided to invest most deeply in the relationships that had that potential, and in every case, those friends reciprocated the investment. As months of conversations over coffee, family barbecues, play dates with our kids, prayer and worship sessions, and other shared experiences turned into years, I couldn't help feeling sure that my dreams for community were beginning to come true.

Then our friend and the founder of Jesus Culture, Banning Liebscher, dropped a bomb on all my rosy visions for these growing relationships. He announced that he was moving Jesus Culture from Redding to Sacramento to plant a church. We immediately knew we were supposed to go with him—not out of duty or obligation, but because we felt God moving our hearts to continue partnering with Banning and his vision. Banning had always given Chris a stage where he could share his passion, and had supported us for years as a wonderful leader and employer. We trusted him and wanted to be part of what God was calling him and Jesus Culture to do.

Despite all the confirmation that moving to Sacramento was what God had planned for our future, however, the idea of moving again did not excite me at all. I had pictured myself growing old and gray in Redding, and my children growing old and gray in Redding! The thought of giving up this dream was confusing and disappointing. I had to spend some time working through these emotions with the Lord before I could start to feel some hope that I would be able maintain some of the relationships I'd built in Redding and develop more friendships in Sacramento.

One of the challenging dynamics in this season of transition, however, was that it was a time of exponential growth for Jesus Culture, which meant that my husband's public platform and popularity were rapidly expanding. In the few years leading up to the church plant, Jesus Culture conferences, tours, album releases, and other projects and events Chris was leading or collaborating on were constantly increasing in number and size. In the meantime, I had been working on my own social media projects around fitness and nutrition for moms, and had been gaining more and more followers—in part because people recognized me as Chris's wife.

I had never really been in any kind of spotlight before, and feeling it just as I was moving to a new city made me even more anxious about making friends. Would the people I met in Sacramento judge me? What if I wasn't as awesome as I seemed to them on social media? What if I made my husband look bad? I know this probably sounds melodramatic, as I'm hardly a celebrity, but it was just strange to encounter more and more people who knew me as the wife of a popular Christian music artist, and seemed to have preconceived ideas about me. I began to experience a level of insecurity I hadn't felt since my teenage years. I became so worried that everyone I met already had an opinion of me before I even opened my mouth that I started to shut down and hide at home. Instead of trying to get to know the women I met in Sacramento, I kept myself at a distance, wishing there was an easy shortcut to finding trustworthy friends who truly wanted to know me. I did my best to fill my friendship cup with occasional phone calls and visits with my best friend in Redding.

Then we lost Jet. I don't know how long I would have kept hiding in my insecurities if that had never happened, but when it did, I couldn't hide anymore. Neither Chris nor I had ever walked through a loss like that in our lives, and we found ourselves desperately needing and experiencing the gift of our community in a way we never had. The outpouring of love and support from our friends, family, and church families in both Redding and Sacramento was truly tremendous. I can't imagine what it would have been like to try to survive that season without their prayers, comfort, generosity, kindness, and understanding.

STRONGER TOGETHER

Walking through this needy, vulnerable time of mourning brought a few truths home to my heart. First, there is no question that we all need community like we need food, water, and shelter. It's not an option—we simply can't survive without it. The Bible never says, "You can do it all alone!" Instead it says:

> *Two people are better off than one, for they can help each other succeed. If one person falls, the other can reach out and help. But someone who falls alone is in real trouble. Likewise, two people lying close together can keep each other warm. But how can one be warm alone? A person standing alone can be attacked and defeated, but two can stand back-to-back and conquer. Three are even better, for a triple-braided cord is not easily broken.* (Ecclesiastes 4:9-12)

Second, I realized that while long-distance relationships are valuable, we need friendships with people who can share our lives more frequently than once every month or so. As I mourned and processed and faced the demands of each new day, it became clear to me that I needed local friends, not just my best friends in other cities who I called or FaceTimed when I wanted to talk. I needed people to do life with, people who could see me on the high days and the low days and share laughter and tears.

Lastly, my season of mourning showed me how much the people around me could affect me, which brought greater focus to what I was looking for in close friendships. The pain of grief puts you in a vulnerable, sensitive place. When pain, sadness, fear, or anger are making it difficult for you to hold on to hope, remember what is true, or focus on things outside you, the attitudes of the people near you can either help you climb out of that hole, or dig it deeper. I realized I needed to choose friends who shared my commitment to trusting God and proclaiming His goodness in the midst of pain and heartbreak. I wanted friends who were focused on God and those around them, and who demonstrated the qualities I wanted to grow in myself—empathy, humility, respect, and hope. These were the kind of women I had always been attracted to, but now I was willing to put aside my insecurities and pursue them.

As of this writing, I'm happy to say that I have formed new friendships with a handful of wonderful women here in Sacramento. These, along with my best friend in Redding, have and continue to be amazing answers to my prayers and hopes for friendships. While each of them has the character and values described above, they are all completely different from each other and from me, and I love that! I need to be around people who have different perspectives and say things in a way I wouldn't—it keeps my eyes open to God. I can only hope that we will continue to grow together and be there for one another in both joy and grief.

IT'S OKAY TO BE PICKY

I know some people feel a little uncomfortable with this whole idea of choosing friends, because it sounds like you're being exclusive. And you are!

However, being exclusive when it comes to deciding who gets to know you intimately is not a bad thing. It's actually right and appropriate. Like marriage, a friendship is a mutual relationship with a heart-to-heart connection or soul tie. When you have this kind of connection with someone, it means that you have given them access to a deep level of knowledge and influence in your life. The Bible tells us to choose our friends carefully because of how they can influence us:

> *He who walks with wise men will be wise,*
> *But the companion of fools will suffer harm.*
> (Proverbs 13:20)

> *Do not associate with a man given to anger; Or*
> *go with a hot-tempered man, Or you will learn*
> *his ways And find a snare for yourself.*
> (Proverbs 22:24-25)

> *...for "bad company corrupts good character."*
> (1 Corinthians 15:33)

Many believers have weakened their faith and character and compromised their lives because they chose friendships with people around who were not loyal to Jesus. On the other hand, many other believers have compromised their lives by trying to walk in independence and isolation! Both cases prove the point: If we want to stay faithful to Him and to the truth He has called us to walk in, then we need to be careful to find friends who are likeminded and like-hearted in their pursuit of the Lord. None of us can do this alone. We need people who can speak to us on a heart level, remind us of who we are when we forget, and bring wisdom and courage to us as we face the challenges of each season.

If you struggle with insecurity and fear of rejection that keep you from building these friendships in your life, I encourage you to go to the Lord and ask Him to heal you and bring you godly friends. I realize that relational hurts are often the deepest and most enduring. On the other hand, God brings lasting health and healing to our lives through relationships, because that's how He designed us. He made us for intimacy and connection with Him and others. I also recommend that you take advantage of the great resources that are available to educate yourself on what healthy relationships look like and how to cultivate them. The classic book *Boundaries* by Cloud and Townsend is a great one to check out, as is Danny Silk's *Keep Your Love On!*

While I'm still on a learning journey about how to be a good friend and choose good friends, I've found that it's been helpful to remind myself of a few things as I build relationships. It's always good to believe the best about people and not make quick judgments about someone's character. However, I do pay attention to a person's attitude and how they treat people. Do they gossip, or do they think the best of other friends? Are they disrespectful, or do they show a high value and respect for people's thoughts, feelings, and needs? Do they blame and complain when things don't go their way, or do they demonstrate forgiveness and gratitude? Do they pull away from relationships when they feel insecure, or do they move towards others with vulnerability? These are the kind of questions that help me discern whether it's safe to trust people with my heart.

I also try to carry as much grace, mercy, and forgiveness for my friends as I hope they carry for me. In every relationship, there will be times when we hurt or disappoint one another. None of us will bring the best version of ourselves to the table every single day. Instead of seeing a friend's problems or brokenness as reasons to move away from them, I want to choose to move towards my friends, just as God does. When I make a mess, He doesn't cut me off; He lovingly confronts me, comforts me, and helps me clean it up. That's the kind of friend I need, and want to be.

Chapter 10

RECEIVING HIS GIFTS

The land you have given me is a pleasant land.
What a wonderful inheritance!

PSALM 16:6

When you lose someone you love, especially one whose life was seemingly cut short, it can be tempting to frame every memory and thought about that person in terms of what is missing, irretrievable, or never to be. If I had let myself wander down that dark path, I could have gotten lost in a fantasy of the life we will never spend with Jet. I could have chosen to allow every birthday party, Thanksgiving dinner, and Christmas morning to be overshadowed by the fact that he wasn't there with us. I could have let the thing that was taken from me take me out—out of fully living with joy, hope, and love.

But I haven't, and I won't. There are a thousand reasons why, but they all come down to this: *Life is a gift*. Every life, even the shortest, is a good gift from a good God, and deserves to be treated with gratitude and honor.

Jet's life was a gift to us. Though we will certainly miss him at birthdays, Christmas, and Thanksgiving, we will remember where he is—with the Father, in joy. And we will honor the gift of his life by cherishing the gifts of our lives, and by opening our hearts to more gifts.

Fairly soon after we said goodbye to Jet, Chris and I began talking about whether or not we wanted to try to have another child. The only reason I felt ready to have that conversation right away was because of a moment I had in the hospital shortly after I was induced for Jet's labor. In the midst of my shock, grief, and longing for my son, I was surprised to find another longing stirring inside me. I realized I wanted more children. In fact, I had a strange, instinctive feeling that I would be pregnant again not once, but twice! This feeling surprised me, because I had firmly decided that I only wanted three children. I was also exhausted from my pregnancy with Jet and in no mood to think about being pregnant again. Yet I couldn't shake the desire and conviction for the precious gift of more children in our family.

Eight weeks after Jet's memorial, I took a pregnancy test and learned that I was pregnant with our fourth child. Sure enough, the months of this pregnancy—which have coincided with the writing of this book—have landed me in a space where I get to choose again and again to be thankful, to submit my fears to God, to surrender control, and to carry hope. I get to choose to embrace not only the gift of another new life inside me, but also my own life. Above all, I get to trust that the Giver is good, that He only gives good gifts, that He keeps His promises, and that He knew what He was doing when He gave each of us the life He did.

RECEIVING YOUR LIFE

For some reason, one of the hardest things for us to do as human beings is to receive the gift of our lives. Even those of us who claim to believe truths that give our lives the highest value imaginable— that we are made in God's image, that He paid the greatest price to restore us to that image in Christ, and that He loves and delights in us unconditionally—still struggle to line our thoughts and behavior up with these truths. Christians are often just as good as anyone else, or even better, at looking at our lives through a lens of shame, guilt, and judgment.

Imagine going to an art gallery, seeing a painting, and immediately starting to abuse it: "Oh, please. I can't even believe this is called art. It's horrible. I can see ten different flaws just standing here and looking at it for thirty seconds. What a piece of ugly, worthless junk." Then, in the next breath, you start to praise the artist: "He is a total genius. Flawless work. He simply can't create anything that's less than stunning and perfect." That sounds a little crazy, right? Both of these things cannot be true. You're either wrong about the art or wrong about the artist.

Crazy enough, this is exactly what we do when we praise God for His perfection and creativity in making the world, yet beat ourselves up and belittle our own worth throughout the day. Can you imagine how hurtful that must be for the heart of God? He says that all of His works are beautifully and wonderfully made, yet we don't know how to receive that compliment for ourselves.

Part of the problem, I think, is that some of what we call "humility" in the church is actually just the opposite. Devaluing and diminishing ourselves isn't humility—at its root, it's actually unbelief, idolatry, and pride. That may sound harsh, but it's true. It's elevating our own negative opinions above God's opinions. It's choosing to focus on ourselves and how messed up we are instead of focusing on God. True humility, in contrast, surrenders our right to define ourselves, positively or negatively, by anything but what God says. True humility believes God when He says we are blameless in His sight, acceptable, pure, lovely, and deeply loved. True humility acknowledges both the Giver and His gifts to be *good*, and confidently delights in and uses those gifts in order to glorify the Giver.

It saddens me when Christians call other Christians prideful or arrogant because they allowed the gift of their life to shine in some way. To me, there is nothing more attractive than people who know they are beautiful and blameless in the eyes of God *and* man and generously share their lives with those around them. With that said, however, I confess that it's not always easy for me to make the daily choice to see my life through the lens of what God says about me. Wonderfully, the gift of daughters regularly reminds me what's at stake in my choice not to cut myself or others down, but instead to stand in the truth of my beauty and blamelessness. Whatever I choose is what my girls will learn to choose.

Halfway through this pregnancy, I began feeling especially insecure about my body. While I hadn't gained an especially significant amount of weight, and though I had already been through this process three times before, it was still uncomfortable to watch my body morph once again from muscular and lean (I'm a Pilates and Spin instructor when I'm not pregnant) into a soft and curvy shape, complete with stretch marks and cellulite. If you have had babies, I know you understand how shocking it can be to watch your body get pudgy so quickly!

I was in my bedroom one day, trying on a pile of different clothes, looking for absolutely anything to fit my bloated waistline and my hips, which seemed to have widened overnight. Without realizing, I was mumbling and complaining out loud to myself about how chunky I felt— "Nothing fits me. Errghhh, my butt has gotten way too big for these shorts...when did my thighs get so jiggly?"

Suddenly, I heard a tiny voice behind me say, "My dress looks silly on me. I think I should change. The other kids at school will probably think it doesn't look good on me." My five-year-old, Ella, had witnessed my entire rant about how nothing looked good on me. Because I'm the loudest voice in her life, she immediately aligned with my insecurity and began to pick herself apart.

It broke my heart to see my daughter second-guessing her beauty due to my lack of confidence. I quickly put on an outfit without looking twice in the mirror, got on eye level with my gorgeous, blue-eyed princess, and told her that her dress looked absolutely marvelous. I told her I was so sorry for saying those bad things about myself, because they weren't true. I told her that I know I'm beautiful because God made me perfectly, just like He made her perfectly.

As I shared this simple and childlike lesson about how we are fearfully and wonderfully made, it was obvious to me that I needed to hear it at least as much as my daughter. In fact, I think we never stop needing to hear it. We are saturated by a culture in which people stand in front of the mirror and beat themselves up, then turn around and spend a ton of time and money trying to perfect themselves and attract "likes" on social media to give them a sense of worth. The only people who will turn the tide are those who can turn from the mirror and say, "I am a gift, and so are you. Let's receive these gifts with joy, and offer them to others with joy."

THE TRUTH SETS US FREE

We cannot receive the gift of our lives and honor the Giver without allowing His voice to be loudest and His opinion to define our identity and value. His opinion is the only one that is true, and only the truth can set us free to be who He created us to be and live the life He gave us to live. Whenever we look to human opinion or circumstances to define us, we will only multiply insecurity and bondage in our lives. Conversely, when we look to His opinion, we can be free to be ourselves no matter what others think or what is going on in our circumstances!

In fact, one of the mysteries we discover in experiences of loss is that difficult circumstances can be the best conditions in which to grow in freedom. In *Man's Search for Meaning*, Viktor Frankl describes living through what most of us would consider the worst circumstance we could experience. He and the other prisoners in the concentration camp were not only subjected to physical deprivation, but also to dehumanization, humiliation, and other forms of psychological and emotional trauma. Yet, Frankl wrote, these circumstances only served to give them continuous opportunities to use the thing that could not be taken from them—their freedom:

> Every day, every hour, offered the opportunity to make a decision, a decision which determined whether you would or would not submit to those powers which threatened to rob you of your very self, your inner freedom; which determined whether or not you would become the plaything of circumstance.[10]

When everything is stripped from us, we still have something left: a free choice to be controlled and defined by our circumstances, or by something else. However, I don't believe we need to end up in a concentration camp in order to have the chance to make a free choice not to be the "plaything of

---

[10] Frankl, 75.

circumstance." We can make that free choice in any circumstance—whether we're well fed and happy, or hungry and sad—simply by choosing to be defined by God's voice and opinion and finding our security in Him alone.

THE CLOAK OF SECURITY

When Jacob gave his son Joseph the coat of many colors, it wasn't to make his other sons feel bad. He gave it to Joseph *for* Joseph, not for anyone else. It was a sign that said, "I see who you are, and I favor you because of who you are." Similarly, I believe the Father wants to give us a *cloak of security* that continually reminds us, "I am chosen. I am called. I am free. I am loved. I am a whole and healed being." As we step into our tomorrows, which will surely filled with as many surprises, shocks, and unexpected variables as with things we had planned, we must learn to walk in our Father's cloak of security in every circumstance.

The best lesson I've learned in my entire life has been to remember who I am and how He chose me. Somehow, holding on to these two things makes the puzzle pieces of any circumstance—even suffering and loss—fit together. I'm able to love those who need to be loved, because I know that I myself am loved. I'm able to accept that I'm not being punished by God when something bad happens, and display that to others who blame themselves after tragedy or heartbreak. I'm able to unconditionally love God just as He unconditionally loves me—not based on how many blessings He does or doesn't send my way, but based on His ultimate gift of love.

Every gift of God, including the gift of our lives, is a gift of His love. Every one of us is here on the planet for one sole reason—because God loves us. When we get to heaven, it won't surprise me if, when we ask God all our hard questions about why some things happened and others didn't, He simply answers, "I love you." And that will be enough.

His love mends us. It fills every loss and casts out every fear. Because of His love, tomorrow isn't a day I dread, but a day that I look forward to with my eyes wide open. No matter what lies ahead, I will be steadfast in offering Him the gift of my life as He has offered Himself to me.

Epilogue

USE YOUR MOMENT WELL

When I felt a contraction on the morning of September 16, 2015, I notice that it was pretty strong, but dismissed it as soon as it had subsided. Being thirty-three weeks (seven-and-a-half months) pregnant with our fourth child, a little girl, I had already begun to experience "practice" contractions and other early labor signs. Just two weeks earlier, in fact, I had gone to the ER to double-check whether the contractions I was experiencing were cause for concern. The doctor had assured me they were perfectly normal. If the contractions became stronger and more consistent, he said, I was to rest and drink lots of water until they calmed down.

I fed and dressed Ella and Aria, loaded them into double stroller, and made the two-block walk to drop off Ella at her kindergarten classroom. On the way home, I felt several more contractions. As soon as I reached the house, I poured myself a huge glass of water and snuggled up with Aria on the couch, trusting that would do the trick.

Two hours later, however, the contractions were still coming with the same intensity three to five minutes apart, and I was starting to worry. I had never had painful contractions like this so early in a pregnancy. Telling myself not to panic, I decided the best plan was stay on the couch—all day, if necessary—and do nothing that might aggravate the contractions further. I texted my husband, explained the situation, and asked him to come home

When I felt a contraction on the morning of September 16, 2015, I notice that it was pretty strong, but dismissed it as soon as it had subsided. Being thirty-three weeks (seven-and-a-half months) pregnant with our fourth child, a little girl, I had already begun to experience "practice" contractions and other early labor signs. Just two weeks earlier, in fact, I had gone to the ER to double-check whether the contractions I was experiencing were cause for concern. The doctor had assured me they were perfectly normal. If the contractions became stronger and more consistent, he said, I was to rest and drink lots of water until they calmed down.

I fed and dressed Ella and Aria, loaded them into double stroller, and made the two-block walk to drop off Ella at her kindergarten classroom. On the way home, I felt several more contractions. As soon as I reached the house, I poured myself a huge glass of water and snuggled up with Aria on the couch, trusting that would do the trick.

Two hours later, however, the contractions were still coming with the same intensity three to five minutes apart, and I was starting to worry. I had never had painful contractions like this so early in a pregnancy. Telling myself not to panic, I decided the best plan was stay on the couch— all day, if necessary—and do nothing that might aggravate the contractions further. I texted my husband, explained the situation, and asked him to come home from work, as I wouldn't be able to get anything done around the house.

Chris took care of the girls and played housewife for me while I lay on the couch. As the day wore on with no changes in the contractions, we began saying prayers together for the peace and safety of our child. Then, around 10 p.m., the contractions became even more painful, and I finally admitted that we should probably go to the hospital. I had been putting it off all day—I just didn't want to go back again and be told everything was completely fine.

As Chris and I began packing things up to head to the ER, I suddenly realized something. Just nine months before this, I had been exactly thirty-weeks pregnant with Jet. During that very week, he had died in my womb.

In an instant, paralyzing fear swept through my body. I crumpled to the floor, crying inconsolably and shaking with anxiety. Chris rushed to hold me, quietly repeating that our baby was going to be fine and praying for God's peace to come. Gradually, I managed to calm down, join him in prayer, and allow God's peace to settle in my heart. Pulling myself together, I got up and finished getting ready to head to the ER.

Throughout the forty-minute drive to the hospital, I struggled to take deep breaths and remain composed. I just couldn't help having flashbacks of that same drive nine months before. The terrible words kept echoing through my mind and causing my chest to constrict: *Your son has no heartbeat.*

As we arrived at the hospital and made our way to the Labor and Delivery ward, I braced myself to hear those same words said about my daughter. But when I lay back and the nurse strapped a heartbeat monitor to my belly, the strong, steady thumping of our baby girl's heart came through loud and clear. Tears of joy spilled over and I breathed an enormous sigh of relief.

Suddenly, I heard the doctor examining me saying, "Her feet are coming out. Your baby is in a standing breech position. We need to perform an emergency C-section!"

My mind was reeling. *What? I'm only seven months pregnant! Sure, I've been having contractions, but not anything close to hard labor. How could it be that she is almost out?*

Utterly confused, I asked the doctor why he wanted to perform a C-Section when this had been my easiest labor yet. He briefly explained that since our baby was so tiny, she was at risk for decapitation if delivered in a breech position. Obviously, that was all he needed to say. I begged him to hurry up and get her out!

It took fifteen minutes for the hospital staff to wheel me into an operating room, strap me down, anesthetize my abdomen, and begin to perform the C-section. As I watched and waited, the only thing I could think about was what it would be like to hear my baby girl's first cry. I had been dreaming of hearing that cry throughout the entire pregnancy. The silence in the room after my final push in laboring for Jet had hurt in ways I can't describe. Silently, I prayed to God that I would have that moment again, that I would hear our little girl belting out her first cry with strength and passion.

As the seconds ticked by, I lay frozen, clutching Chris's hand and listening with everything in me for my daughter's voice. I craved it like oxygen. The next voice I heard, however, was the doctor's. "She's out! The NICU staff is going to take her and stabilize her."

As one of the NICU doctors left the room cradling a bundle, I turned to Chris and urged, "Go, go, go! Go be with her!" Without a word, he hurried after the doctor, leaving me strapped to the table as the doctors finished stitching me up. I lay there, feeling the pain of silence once again and wondering what it meant. Why hadn't she cried?

Finally, after what seemed more than an hour, Chris and a NICU nurse came back to the operating room holding our perfect baby girl. Her eyes were open, and right away she stared up into my eyes without making a sound.

"Why isn't she crying?" I frantically asked the nurse.

"She's absolutely fine!" the nurse reassured me. "She's just content."

Relaxing at last, I gazed back into the eyes of a promise—God's promise to protect our daughter.

We named her Liv Mercedes Quilala. Liv means "life" in Norwegian, "alive, full of life" in Icelandic, "My God is a vow" in Hebrew, and "protection" in Norse.

Liv was four pounds, two ounces at birth. The doctors told us she would likely need to stay in the NICU for seven weeks before she would be ready to go home. This was devastating news, because it meant leaving my baby at the hospital every evening—the hospital didn't allow parents to stay overnight. It was heartbreaking to go home without her and wrestle with fear for her survival. Each night, I lay awake in bed, staring at her empty bassinet beside my bed, praying and reminding myself yet again that God had promised to protect our baby girl.

Soon, however, joy and hope began to replace my fears as I watched my precious Liv making tremendous leaps in her development. At three days old, she stopped having Bradys (bradycardia)—episodes where her heart rate fell below 80 beats per minute. Most preemies can have these episodes for weeks after delivery. Her breathing tubes were removed only twenty-four hours after she was born. And after just two weeks of practicing with her every day, Liv learned how to breastfeed exclusively, which meant she had no need for a feeding tube!

Liv completely shocked the doctors. Only seventeen days after her birth, they announced that there was no longer any reason for her to be in the hospital. God had truly worked miracle after miracle in her development. Our baby girl came home strong, healthy, and full of life—everything her name means!

THE HEART OF A CHAMPION

The joy of receiving the precious, miraculous gift of Liv Mercedes Quilala into our lives has been greater than Chris and I ever imagined. After walking through the pain of losing our son and choosing over and over to put our whole trust in God, He answered the cry of our hearts by demonstrating His perfect faithfulness, protection, and steadfast love for us. In the place where my heart might have remained shut down in pain, He not only brought healing—He increased my desire for children! As I look to the future—the future of raising my three girls and any other children God gives us, and the heavenly future in which I will know my son—I feel only hope and promise. The Mender of hearts has brought me through tragedy and into joy, and He will bring me through the days that lie ahead—just as He will do for you and all those who trust Him.

As I close these pages, I want to share a letter Chris and I received from Bill Johnson soon after we said goodbye to our beloved Jet. His words brought us invaluable strength as we walked through the weeks and months of grief. Now, as I hold Liv in my arms, their significance has become even deeper and richer. He wrote:

Dear Chris and Alyssa,

The heart of a champion is formed in the Presence, but proven in the trial. The battle you faced for the life of your son was such a trial. It is one you both fought nobly and with much grace. I'm so proud of you, and honored to call you friends. While we would prefer a different outcome, eternity is the best revenge. Having investments in eternity like this is always painful. But they also have a powerful effect on deepening our affection and awareness of Heaven. And that is always good.

God views victory differently than we do. It's not always measured in the problem being defeated. Sometimes it's measured in the fact that after disappointment and loss we set our hearts to seek His face again. David did this after the loss of his son. He worshiped. He knew of the goodness and faithfulness of God and refused to let his own pain distort such a view. It was this approach to life that enabled David to become one of the greatest champions in all of history.

I watched you honor God in a moment that others would use as an excuse to accuse Him, or at best become indifferent towards Him. You wisely resisted such a temptation and instead have given Him praise. It's a rare sacrifice indeed, as we'll never have the chance to give God that kind of offering in heaven because there isn't any pain, confusion, or loss there. You're using your moment well. Thanks. He will honor you for it.

Holding Jethro was one of the greatest honors in my life. We prayed our best, confident in God's kindness, and are now left with the undervalued treasure—mystery. Because He is good, we can trust Him with mystery.

During our time together I caught a glimpse of Jethro in heaven. He was around four or five years old, with black curly hair, running through a field. He was laughing. It felt like that's how he'd look when at the end of your long life you finally meet him. I don't know how that works theologically, nor do I know if it was literal or symbolic. It matters not. He is home. And some day we will be.

Thank you for the privilege of sharing your deepest moment of pain with you. I love you and am proud of you.

Bill Johnson

Of all the prayers I have prayed in writing this book, this one stands above all—that in sharing my story, I would somehow encourage you to *use your moment well*. Whether it's a moment of fullness or a moment of loss, your response today matters not only tomorrow, but in eternity. Will you trust and press in to the goodness of God in this moment? Will you let Him form the heart of a champion in you, a heart formed in the Presence and proven in the trial? Will you invite Him to mend your tomorrows by making a living sacrifice of your life today? With all my heart, I am answering, "Yes!" to these questions—and I hope you will too. I know He will not disappoint us.